RECALL NEWSOM

THE CASE AGAINST AMERICA'S MOST CORRUPT GOVERNOR

KEVIN KILEY

First Edition January 2021
ISBN: 978-X-XX-XXXXXX-X

Cover art by John Adlai
Interior layout by Teddi Deppner
Production by Joshua Hoover

Printed in the United States of America

Published by Kevin Kiley
www.CapitolQuagmire.com

“Power tends to corrupt and absolute power corrupts absolutely.”

– John Dalberg-Acton

ACKNOWLEDGMENTS

The Recall is a citizens' movement, and I want to thank the countless patriotic Californians who have worked tirelessly to bring it to life. Without you, there would not be a book to write. It's because of your heroic efforts that we have this opportunity to set our state on the right course.

This book came together very quickly, and would not have been possible without tremendous support from a number of people. I'm quite lucky in that one of the smartest people I've ever met, John Reynen, is also so generous with his time, providing detailed feedback on every chapter and making sure each argument was not only fully accurate and logically rigorous but a true reflection of the vision we share for our state (while also helping me to keep a sense of humor during long stretches of writing!). John Adlai stepped up and designed a fantastic cover. Teddi Deppner did amazing work getting the book ready for primetime in the final stages of production. On the Recall campaign, thank you in particular to Orrin Heatlie, Mike Netter, and Randy Economy for your encouragement of this project and for working day and night as leaders of the movement.

Thank you to my research team, Blanye Clegg-Swann, Chris Luna, Daniel Lieber, Max Minshull, Megan Myers, and Abigail Scott, for working through the holidays to help make this a book that I believe will stand up to exacting scrutiny. And thank you to Joshua Hoover who ably managed and organized its production, while also exemplifying public service as a leader in our own community. Finally, thank you to my Assembly staff members. They are the best team I could ask for and have helped a great many people in our district weather the storms of this past year.

CONTENTS

PREFACE

A Tale of Two Speeches

On March 16, 2020, I rose to address my colleagues in the California State Assembly.

"Today," I began, "I am supporting our Governor. I call on every legislator and every Californian, regardless of political preference, to trust in Governor Newsom's leadership and listen to his guidance."

I spoke from my desk on the far-left side of the Assembly. The Chamber is a grand, magnificent space, modeled after Britain's House of Commons. I've always enjoyed hosting classes on field trips and seeing the students look around in awe. Above the dais hangs a portrait of Abraham Lincoln holding the Emancipation Proclamation. Sometimes I imagine an animated Honest Abe, like a painting in Harry Potter, musing at the proceedings below as the People's representatives pass legislation to designate an official state sport (surfing), state dinosaur (Augustynolophus morrisi), and even a state nut (almond, pecan, walnut *and* pistachio—as it turns out, all technically seeds).

But frivolity is not usually the reason I imagine our 16th President to be shaking his painted head. More commonly, it's something much worse: corruption. Lincoln must have encountered his share of it as an Illinois state representative in the 1830s. But there is no comparison, past or present, to what happens underneath the dome of the California State Capitol.

When I rise to give a speech in the Assembly, it is usually to oppose some corrupt scheme that Special Interests have cooked up, to be rubber stamped by their legislative enablers. Sometimes I succeed in killing such legislation, but more often what is said on the Assembly Floor doesn't matter. The outcome is preordained; debate is nonexistent or farcical. Whenever I speak, the Majority Leader is on guard to try to find ways to cut me off. Every year, new methods are devised to stifle discussion and public participation.

The contrast could not be greater between the grandeur of the Assembly Chamber and the tawdriness of its proceedings. Observers are often taken aback by the absence of any apparent sense of responsibility or public mindedness in this room where 80 men and women are trusted with matters of profound importance to 40 million people. Yet on this day, March 16, I hoped it would be different. I tried to summon a sense of our collective responsibility as we faced an impending crisis.

"I rise today at a moment without precedent in any of our experience," I said. "For nearly 40 million Californians, 330 million Americans, and people around the world, this is a surreal time, a sharp and sudden break from all normalcy. It's a moment of crisis in every sense—social paralysis, economic upheaval, and mortal peril. The partisan rituals of ordinary politics have no place in these extraordinary times."

Now, even at this moment, I was no fan of Gavin Newsom. In his first year in office, I watched him hand over the keys to the Governor's Office to Special Interests that spent millions electing him. He signed one of the most corrupt laws ever passed in the United States, Assembly Bill 5, which put tens of thousands of independent contractors out of work. He viciously went after our poorest kids by seeking to close the public schools that serve them best. He'd proven the very embodiment of our Capitol's corruption. And unlike his predecessor Jerry Brown, who made an effort to build relationships with legislators, Newsom seemed to find it beneath him. Even favorable media outlets gave his first year poor reviews.

But none of that mattered to me on March 16. Our state faced a novel threat, and Newsom was our Governor. We needed to work together. From my desk in the Assembly I called on our state's elected leaders to put aside any differences.

"A relationship of trust, openness, dialogue, and accessibility between Californians and their elected representatives has never been more important," I said. "We're in this together, and the only way we can meet these challenges is together—with ingenuity and resourcefulness, with goodwill and compassion, with strength and solidarity. Social distance need not mean societal dissonance, or spiritual discord. In a way, the very interconnectedness that made this virus so quick to spread also gives us the capacity to defeat it."

The essence of political leadership, in my view, is bringing people together for a shared purpose. Beyond the griminess and sharp edges, the practice of politics can appeal to the better angels of our nature (in Lincoln's memorable words) as we pursue something larger than ourselves. This is what I hoped our Governor would do at this uncertain moment in our state's history.

My own background was not a political one. I had worked as a high school teacher in inner-city Los Angeles and later as a prosecutor. I left behind a promising career in the private sector to run for office because I saw the corruption of our state's politics causing its steady and seemingly irreversible decline. I sensed this was linked to the erosion of government by the people and the toxicity of our political culture. As of this day in March, I had spent three years fighting for change at the Capitol—an uphill battle if there ever was one. But I thought perhaps the common threat posed by the novel coronavirus would allow us to see ourselves as one people again, to reclaim a distinctive state spirit that was drifting away.

"We have another advantage," I said, "a can-do sense of possibility that is distinctly Californian—an unmatched ability to take our circumstances and make the best of them. That's what we must do, now more than ever. Whether we can rise to the occasion in the days and weeks ahead will determine the fate of untold lives and will shape what our state looks like on the other side."

I could not have imagined that almost a year later, the other side would still be out of sight. Nor could I have known that for most of the year, Abraham Lincoln would have the Assembly Chamber to himself. The Legislature decided to simply stop working, while at the other end of the Capitol, in a ring of offices known as the Horseshoe, Governor Gavin Newsom was all-too present.

* * *

Nearly nine months after that speech, on December 7, 2020, I addressed the State Assembly again. This was the one and only day the Legislature was in session over a span of four and a half months. We met not in the august Assembly Chamber but, for social distancing reasons, down the street at the Golden One basketball arena—home of a Sacramento Kings team I've been cursed with rooting for my whole life. It was, to put it mildly, a very different setting for a very different speech.

"When I addressed this Assembly on March 16, I said the partisan rituals of ordinary politics have no place in these extraordinary times. I called on every legislator and every Californian, regardless of political preference, to trust in Governor Newsom's leadership and listen to his guidance.

"Gavin Newsom made a mockery of that trust. Within weeks, he hid from the Legislature a $1 billion no-bid deal with a political ally, outsourced the most important decisions to powerful Special Interests, and started talking about using the coronavirus as an opportunity for a 'new progressive era.'

"But the outcomes have been anything but progressive. Our economy is doing about the worst in the country, our kids in poor communities are faring worst of all, our public health performance is middling. With the basic pillars of a liberal democracy dismantled, our citizenry is disenfranchised and divided.

"The fact is this Governor has lost all credibility with the public. Whatever the shortcomings of this Legislature, in this moment we have one inherent advantage: we are not Gavin Newsom."

***

This book covers the fateful months between those two speeches, as California suffered through the worst COVID-19 response in the country and perhaps the larger Western world.

I tried in every way I could to get Gavin Newsom to govern in the public interest. But instead, he used this moment of utmost vulnerability to promote his own political ambitions and reward his Special Interest benefactors, putting every perversity of California politics on steroids. As Californians rose to the occasion heroically, their Governor let them down repeatedly. "When history called, he flopped," wrote Jerry Brown's Press Secretary, Gil Duran.

Whoever wins a Recall election will certainly have shortcomings, as anyone does. But that person will have the same advantage I told our Legislature we have. He or she will not be Gavin Newsom.

INTRODUCTION

We the People

If you are looking for a book arguing that COVID-19 is a hoax, this is not it. If you are looking for a comprehensive case against lockdowns in general, that is not its purpose. If you are looking for a broadside against liberal policies, there are plenty of other such books available.

This is a book about the distinctive failures of Governor Gavin Newsom, who has mismanaged the COVID crisis in a way that embodies the endemic corruption of California state government. In the process, he's taken that corruption to new depths—with devastating consequences for millions of people.

I am a Republican, and my political views are readily available elsewhere in the public domain. But this book is not red meat for partisans. It is meant for liberal Democrats just as much as conservative Republicans. In these pages, I do not advocate for any particular policies; I simply oppose those which result from corruption. That is because I do not believe that political disagreement over policies or values is enough for a recall. We hash out those differences in regularly scheduled elections. In fact, I was skeptical of the 2003 Gray Davis Recall, even though I was no supporter of Davis himself.

That's one reason I am writing this book: I am generally *recall reluctant*. I also believe that recalls, as a tool for throwing out politicians, should not be led by politicians themselves. They should be citizens' movements. When I first met the Lead Proponent of the Newsom Recall, Orrin Heatlie, it was February 2020. Over coffee at

Bill's Donuts in Granite Bay, I told him I wished him luck and admired his efforts to mobilize Californians seeking change, but that I could not lend my support to the Recall at that time—as much as I would have liked to see Governor Newsom out of office.

While our Constitution allows a recall to be initiated for any reason, for me to support one three criteria must be met. First, a recall should respond to a betrayal of the public trust—the use of power vested in the officeholder for purposes other than the solemn duties of the office. Second, a recall should respond to a need for fundamental change. Finally, a recall should be a last resort.

At the time of this writing in January 2021, I believe all three criteria have been abundantly met. And Orrin Heatlie along with countless others have built what is truly a citizens' movement in every sense. I am writing this book to promote *their* efforts, in a supporting role. They are the lead actors.

A Betrayal of the Public Trust

Even standard corruption like that on display during Newsom's first year—or every day in our Legislature—would not be grounds for me to actively support a recall. What is exceptional about Gavin Newsom's COVID era performance is the pernicious combination of corruption and lawlessness. He has compromised our institutions of self-government—the rule of law, checks and balances, separation of powers, representative democracy, and the Constitution itself—to promote himself and the cash-flush Special Interests that put him in office. It is Newsom's abuse of extraordinary emergency powers for personal political gain, with a totalizing impact on California life, that makes this the most meritorious recall in our state's history.

In the pages that follow, I will discuss how Governor Newsom has betrayed the public trust in ways without equal in the United States today or in the history of California. In particular, Part II identifies the eight defining characteristics of Newsom's worst-in-the-nation COVID response.

Self-promotional: Soon after declaring a State of Emergency, Newsom began making far-reaching decisions based more on what would garner him press coverage than what would protect Californians. As he made the rounds on daytime and late-night talk shows, he pursued increasingly dishonest, damaging, and desperate ploys to compete with New York Governor Andrew Cuomo for national attention. To many observers, Newsom treated the arrival of the coronavirus on our shores as the launch of his 2024 presidential campaign.

Lawless: To get his name in the headlines as quickly as possible, Newsom fashioned himself in the mold of an ancient Roman dictator, falsely claiming the emergency "centralized the State's powers" in his hands. He changed over 400 laws by fiat, created entirely new law unrelated to public health, and left Californians without a voice in their own government. He repeatedly clashed with lawmakers of both parties as he refused to stop acting unilaterally. I prosecuted the legal case against the Governor along with my fellow legislator James Gallagher, and in a seminal decision, a California Superior Court ruled the Governor had abused his emergency powers and repeatedly violated the California Constitution.

Corrupt: Newsom has used the State of Emergency to richly reward the Special Interests that spent millions electing him and whose favor he would need to run for higher office. He appointed the nation's single largest partisan donor, vanity presidential candidate Tom Steyer, to head California's economic recovery. At the behest of his biggest benefactor, the California Teachers Association, he kept schools closed as long as any state, doing incalculable harm to millions of kids. He devoted scarce budget dollars to enforce AB 5 in order to increase profits for massive union conglomerates. He became so ensnared with lobbyists that he was forced to appoint a "Chief Ethics Advisor."

Unscientific: Because it was driven by politics and self-interest, the Governor's COVID response has been denounced by health experts as unscientific, counterproductive, and not based on data. Newsom repeatedly refused to provide evidence for his shutdown orders, and multiple courts found there to be none. He haphazardly changed the rules time and again without a coherent explanation. Unlike any governor, he imposed lockdowns for non-health reasons, such as "equity." He enforced bans on activities such as outdoor dining, bowling, youth sports, and playgrounds that virtually no other state did. Newsom even put up barriers to a vaccine in order to make a political statement.

Partisan: From the beginning, Newsom celebrated COVID-19 as the dawning of a "new progressive era," as "an opportunity to reshape the way we do business and how we govern." Already America's most partisan governor, Newsom took his divisiveness to perverse levels when he released a spurious chart purporting to rank "red" and "blue" states by COVID cases. Even as our state's problems mounted, he spent his time trolling United States Senators, comparing the leader of the Senate to a "jellyfish, coral, slug, snail, or octopus," and posting a fake news video about a U.S. Supreme Court nominee that he was forced to delete.

Hypocritical: Newsom will always be remembered for sitting at a crowded table, without a mask, to fete a lobbyist at a meal with a $12,000 wine bill at a time he was forcing Californians to stay home and failing to deliver the modest unemployment checks they were owed. But the French Laundry scandal only scratched the surface of Newsom's hypocrisy. He sent his own children to private school for in-person instruction even as he forced millions of less fortunate kids to learn from home. He repeatedly blamed the people of California for the spread of the virus even as he asked them to make pointless sacrifices not linked to public health. He spoke of equity and inclusiveness while taking actions that were an assault on those values.

Incompetent: Newsom oversaw the country's worst and most Orwellian unemployment office, which has kept millions of deserving Californians waiting for benefits as billions flew out the door to prisoners posing as claimants. Newsom used agency personnel to harass small business owners with audits and required independent contractors to name names of business partners who could be harassed with audits of their own. Newsom also neglected basic preparations for California's data systems, leading to a major data "glitch," after which he disappeared for a week before accepting the resignation of his public health director. To avoid accountability, the Governor repeatedly directed self-investigations of his own Administration and denied information to the public.

Neglectful: Amid Newsom's publicity-seeking and political-calculating, he neglected the basics of a public health response. California was among the slowest states in the country to ramp up testing. Newsom refused to allow testing at pharmacies and failed to sufficiently develop contact tracing tools. He did not do what was needed to protect vulnerable populations, and despite the urgent warnings of a Democratic lawmaker, presided over the "worst prison health screw up in state history." He kept in place Special Interest-backed barriers to working on the healthcare front lines and, amid a record surge in cases, did not utilize 99.979 percent of workers who had signed up for the California Health Corps.

The results of these betrayals of the public trust speak for themselves. While California had imposed the nation's strictest lockdown and most sweeping school closures, at the time of this writing it had the most new COVID cases per capita in the country in addition to nearly the worst unemployment rate. It is difficult to imagine a more consequential failure of political leadership.

A Need for Fundamental Change

California's problems were boiling over before COVID-19. Despite boasting the world's fifth largest economy, we have up to half the nation's homeless. We also have the highest rate of poverty, nearly the worst income inequality, the highest housing prices, among the worst roads and bridges, and the worst education for poor students in the continental United States. A recent survey showed a staggering 53 percent of residents were thinking of leaving. When over half of your people want out, that's called a failed state.

Consider a few headlines from eclectic news sources in the months leading up to COVID: California Is Becoming Unlivable (The Atlantic). Why Would Anyone Live in California? (Washington Times). It's the End of California as We Know it (New York Times). How Does California Ever Survive? (CalMatters). As Victor Davis Hanson put it, "Our resolute ancestors took a century to turn a wilderness into California. Our irresolute generation in just a decade or two has been turning California into a wilderness."

Gavin Newsom's mishandling of COVID-19 has dramatically accelerated these trends. Sustained double digit unemployment has deepened poverty and inequality. The achievement gaps in our schools, already disgraceful, have grown considerably. And Californians now sense that the American dream is dead: In a recent poll, nearly two-thirds say kids growing up in California today will be worse off than their parents. Adding further clarity to this picture, data released in December shows California just had its worst population growth in a century, losing a net 135,600 people to other states. Mark Baldassare with the nonpartisan Public Policy Institute of California called the numbers "really startling," saying, "This isn't the Golden State of the past," where people came from all over "to find their way to the California dream."

Our state's inherent beauty and countless wonders, our population's peerless aptitude and esprits de corps, are being overwhelmed by the failure of our politics. And that failure has a specific cause: the capture of our State Capitol.

California's Capitol is not truly run by elected representatives, but by what's known as the "Third House." That's the term for a corps of Special Interest lobbyists, with offices encircling the Capitol, that accounts for the vast majority of political funding in California. It's called the Third House because these lobbyists control the first two houses, the Assembly and Senate. And they certainly control the Governor. Gavin Newsom's 2022 reelection account has over $19 million, with primary funding from unions, associations, and major corporations with registered lobbyists. Several of these benefactors were around the table at his infamous French Laundry dinner. In fact, the lobbyist being feted that night apparently used his influence to help secure an exemption from Newsom's lockdowns for Hollywood. This is why Newsom's one-man rule has worked out so well for Special Interests.

But it's the same for legislators. The Chair of the Assembly Appropriations Committee raised around $1 million this last election, and just about all of it came from Special Interests. Exactly nine contributions came from actual people; not a single contribution was under $100. Every legislator gets hundreds of thousands of dollars from the Third House. It's easy money, and all other funding pales in comparison. But if you cross the biggest players, they'll spend millions against you in your next election. So they always get their way at the Capitol. That's how Sacramento works—and it's why our state is crumbling. It's also why I refuse all funding from the Third House and am the only 100 percent citizen-backed legislator.

As Special Interests have taken over the State Capitol, what we've lost is our institutions and traditions of self-government—a trend that has also reached a breaking point during the COVID response. While for years the architecture of self-government has been dismantled, brick by brick, in 2020 the entire edifice came crashing down, leaving the people of California trapped in the rubble. For years, local communities have lost ever more power to Sacramento; last year, they lost everything to a single person. For years, public access to policymaking has diminished; last year, it disappeared altogether. For years, state bureaucracies have grown larger and more controlling; last year, they all but took over our lives.

The Recall is thus about something more fundamental than placing a new occupant in the Governor's office. It's about repudiating everything the current occupant stands for. That means restoring government by the people, so Californians are no longer subjects of state power but once again authors of our own political destiny. It means repairing our broken political institutions, so they are capable of reversing our state's decline and saving the California Dream before it's too late.

This kind of fundamental change requires an extraordinary act of popular sovereignty—an emphatic rejection of the status quo by the people of California. That's the only remedy for the corruption at the core of our politics. It's what Bruce Ackerman, in his work *We the People*, refers to as "higher lawmaking," where citizens take action "with a seriousness that they do not normally accord to politics." What results is a kind of "supreme law in the name of the People." Because such acts of higher lawmaking only come from a highly engaged public, they can have lasting significance, setting the terms and defining the political realities for years or even generations to come.

At this moment, the California public has never been more attentive to and dissatisfied with our state government. That creates an opportunity for a transformational act of popular sovereignty. Such a political disruption coming directly from the people could redound far into the future, reshuffling the stacked deck of our political system. And a recall election is well-suited to this form of higher lawmaking: by its nature, it is a clean yes-or-no referendum on the status quo. In fact, the recall procedure was added to the State Constitution in 1911 as a tool to "unlock the special interest grip" on state politics. For a state in need of a fundamental course correction, a recall is the ideal vehicle.

But even a successful recall doesn't bring fundamental change automatically. The reason the Gray Davis Recall failed to fundamentally change our politics is because it was not *driven* by the fundamental failures of our politics. It was simply about an uncompelling politician who was doing his job poorly. He was replaced by a much more compelling politician, but it was merely a personnel change; it did not shift the tectonic plates of our political system.

In the same vein, opposing Gavin Newsom for reelection in 2022 would not be the same as a recall. For one thing, Newsom would have another two years to abuse the public trust and hasten our state's decline. For another, in a normal election Special Interests are more adapted to blocking change; indeed, every California governor since 1942 has won a new term. But finally, even a Newsom defeat would signal an ordinary transfer of political power, not the extraordinary act of popular sovereignty that this moment demands.

A Last Resort

A recall is not a remedy I turn to lightly. It is far from the first intervention I have pursued. In my speech on March 16, I asked all legislators and all Californians to trust in Governor Newsom's leadership. In the early days of the crisis, I went out of my way to applaud actions I agreed with and encourage him wherever I could. Even as I implored the Governor to change course in a number of areas, I withheld public criticism as much as possible and was generally supportive.

But as days turned to weeks, it became impossible to hold back criticism consistent with my own responsibilities to the public. There was less and less to applaud, more and more to be alarmed by. The Governor started not merely responding to the public health emergency but ruling the state by decree in ways unrelated to any pandemic. In early May, Assemblyman Gallagher and I tried to engage the Governor in a dialogue about the scope of his emergency powers. His response was to deputize his Legislative Affairs Secretary to falsely accuse us of trying to "to prematurely declare an end to this ongoing crisis that has killed nearly 100,000 Americans." He has repeatedly resorted to these kinds of demagogic statements, all the while falsely claiming that a State of Emergency turns California into an autocracy until he says otherwise.

Since Newsom refused to cooperate or acknowledge any limits on his powers, we took him to court. After we defeated him once, I publicly proposed conditions for "a more constructive and cooperative relationship" between our two branches of government, which included the Governor involving the Legislature in the enactment of further Executive Orders and acknowledging that there were limits to his emergency powers. Instead of engaging with this proposal, he had the judge who ruled against him removed from our case. After we defeated him again at the trial, his response was to rush to the Court of Appeal to seek an "extraordinary writ."

As another example, before the Governor issued his school closure order in July, I strongly urged him to follow the science and let schools stay open. Just days earlier that had been his position, too. But then his top campaign benefactor weighed in and Newsom did a 180, ignoring my advice and ordering almost all schools in the state closed. I have since highlighted every new piece of evidence showing that keeping schools open is the right thing for students and the right thing for public health. Yet to this day, Newsom is keeping millions of kids out of school against the overwhelming advice of public health authorities, including Dr. Anthony Fauci.

Similarly, Newsom has for months ignored our calls to take a more science-based approach to the virus, and California now leads the nation in new cases. Newsom also refused to address the concerns of dozens of lawmakers about mismanagement at the Employment Development Department, leaving millions of Californians without timely unemployment benefits. Most dishonorably, after I presented him with hundreds of testimonials from people unable to work because of the double whammy of AB 5 and the lockdown orders—including nurses and other healthcare professionals—the Governor not only ignored the cries for help of these desperate Californians but spent millions enforcing the law against them.

It is not just me Newsom has ignored. He has dismissed the entire Legislature. From nearly the beginning, lawmakers in both parties have publicly criticized the Governor for announcing major decisions on television shows without consulting with the Legislature or even informing us beforehand. Senator Holly Mitchell (D-Los Angeles), Chair of the Joint Budget Committee, said, "The Legislature has repeatedly called for the Executive Branch to collaborate on COVID-19 response. But time and again, the Legislature has been put in the position of simply giving a yes or no answer to the Governor's priorities." Assemblyman Phil Ting (D-San Francisco) decried the Governor's "huge overreach of authority" and "disdain to properly communicate with the Legislature," observing that "the governor does not have complete authority to do whatever he wants."

Even prior supporters of the Governor have been alarmed by his refusal to change his ways. In August, the California Opinion Editor for The Sacramento Bee, a paper that endorsed Newsom, wrote, "There's no way to undo the failure, confusion and death of the last few months. But if Newsom can stop thinking like a politician and start acting like a leader, there may be some hope for California yet." By November, the Bee's Editorial Board did not see improvement: "Two years into his first term, and nine months into the COVID-19 pandemic, Newsom still can't get his act together. If Newsom can't get his head into the game, perhaps he should make this governor thing a one-term affair and leave the job open for someone with a desire to lead."

Many of us have tried, in every way possible, to get the Governor to change his self-promotional, lawless, corrupt, unscientific, partisan, incompetent, hypocritical, neglectful COVID-19 response. Yet for 10 months, he has refused, causing grievous and lasting damage to our state.

* * *

If we are to have a true recovery, not only from the nightmare of this past year but from decades of decay, it must rest on a foundation of honesty and decency. That means eschewing partisanship, bringing people together, and returning power to local communities. It means, above all, trusting and respecting the people of California.

The specific policies for a post-Newsom era are not the subject of this book. But Part III touches on the fundamental changes needed to respond to the underlying reasons for the Recall—the institutional repair that will allow us to restore checks and balances, revive self-government, root out corruption, and resume the basic functions of good government.

This past year has brought unimaginable hardship. But the months ahead can produce an epochal moment in our state's history. While a recall is an inherently confrontational event, by breaking free of the nation's most divisive governor, I believe we can come together again as a state. California can once again start leading the nation in the right ways and reclaim what we've always stood for: opportunity, innovation, derring-do, and the singular power of a free people to make tomorrow better than today.

PART I

PRELUDE TO COVID

CHAPTER ONE

The Mario Kart Governor

"The blunders came by wanting press hits so badly to show that he's leading on the national stage." – Top Legislative Staffer, on Newsom's first year as Governor

In December of 2019, Governor Gavin Newsom was looking for a way to memorialize his first year in office. The self-tribute he decided on was a Mario-Kart style animation produced with his own campaign funds and then pinned to the top of his Twitter profile for days.

"You don't need me to tell you that 2019 has been a difficult year for our country," a Newsom voiceover begins, as we see a caricature of President Donald Trump wearing a bright red tie and driving a red go-kart. Newsom narrates that Trump "continued on his horrifying course of attacking our institutions and our fellow Americans" as the cartoon President drives over a copy of the Constitution and wreaks havoc on pedestrians. Trump's "feckless allies in Congress cheered him on," Newsom continues, with caricatures of Mitch McConnell and Paul Ryan cheering like NASCAR fans as the President does a wheelie.

The cartoon President then pulls his go-kart up to the starting line, where he is met by a cartoon Gavin Newsom, wearing a bold blue tie in a blue go-kart. The artist took the liberty of making the President's face implausibly round and droopy while making the Governor's implausibly angular and square-jawed. "In California," Newsom narrates, "We're not letting Trump slow down our progress." The race begins and Newsom gets a jumpstart as the President is busy laughing villainously.

The race proceeds, with Newsom's voiceover describing his various accomplishments as associated obstacles appear on the racetrack. As he hails a bill changing school start times, his avatar's go-kart passes a bus of sleepy students, who light up at the sight of their hero while the bus blocks the President's path. As Newsom boasts of building the first statewide early warning earthquake system, a fault line opens up on the racetrack, which the President crashes into after the Governor sails over it.

Then the animation gets darker. As the voiceover describes legislation giving greater rights to student-athletes, a bald curmudgeonly man driving an NCAA go-kart—and wearing the same red tie as Trump, McConnell, and Ryan—side swipes the kart of a young basketball player. Luckily, Newsom saves the day, firing a shell from behind to blow the older man off the track. Having vanquished this foe, Newsom then grabs a basketball from the athlete and throws it at the President's kart, causing him to crash too. The conquering hero wheels along as other fawning constituents salute him. When the voiceover mentions gun reform, the cartoon Newsom throws a bucket of blue paint on two NRA officials, both wearing red ties.

As the race nears its end, Newsom easily clears a gap in the track that's parallel to the Golden Gate bridge. The President doesn't make it, becoming suspended in midair and then falling to what would surely be a violent death in the water below. But somehow he reappears, only to lose control again when he is pelted by a newspaper hailing Newsom's moratorium on the death penalty.

Yet the two men are still neck-and-neck as the race nears its end. To finish the President off, Newsom throws a banana peel in his path, causing yet another violent crash that dislodges a tire. As his cartoon likeness crosses the finish line in triumph, Newsom narrates: "So what's ahead as we race into 2020? Well we're not taking our foot off the gas, especially when the stakes are this high. Our country is looking to California, and we'll continue leading the way."

* * *

The animation flopped. It got little social media traction and received only one brief mention in news reports. While you might wonder how any elected official could produce something like this and expect to be taken seriously, for Newsom it was par for the course. It was a final, desperate look-at-me gambit to cast what most agreed was a mediocre first year as somehow deserving of the national spotlight. In this way, the animation ironically succeeded in conveying the essence of Newsom's 2019 performance—focused more on getting attention than getting results—and foreshadowed much of what would go so wrong with his COVID-19 response.

In an in-depth article published at the end of 2019, the Los Angeles Times spoke with a number of the Governor's "allies," who "asked for anonymity to speak freely about the governor, fearing repercussions should they be named." The Times reported that "Newsom has struggled with what some critics believe is an undisciplined and impatient governing style." A top legislative staffer said, "For a year in, it still has a chaotic, 'the left hand doesn't know what the right hand is doing' kind of feel to it." In a similar piece, a top staffer told Politico "the Brown administration would be so embarrassed to be off-message" in the way Newsom was. Another Capitol aide said, "I think the feeling right now is you can't trust anything that they say," referring to Newsom and his advisors. All of this led a New York Times columnist to observe that even with a booming economy, "[t]rust and communication between the governor and the Legislature[] frayed."

Some of the Governor's allies went on the record with their criticism.

Kathryn Phillips, director of Sierra Club California, said, "I expected sort of a steadier, more methodical governor. I found the decisions he made, the statements he made, more erratic than expected." She continued: "I think he ended up the year looking like a rank amateur."

White House Dreams

The LA Times year-in-review story quotes a top Capitol staffer bluntly identifying the cause of Newsom's problems: "The blunders came by wanting press hits so badly to show that he's leading on the national stage."

The story lists several examples of Newsom "over hyping announcements," such as "inaccurately" claiming that "his raising of the LGBTQ Pride flag above the Capitol" was a state first or announcing he was moving into the historic Governor's mansion downtown when he had already bought a "six-acre, $3.7-million Fair Oaks compound." Lawmakers also complained that Newsom kept the press more in the loop than them, with one saying of his decision to weaken her proposal to lower taxes on diapers and feminine hygiene products: "I learned about it from the media. It seemed odd." A Politico story likewise emphasized Newsom's tendency for "getting publicly ahead of closed-door realities."

The Sacramento Bee Editorial Board, which had endorsed Newsom for governor, gave him a nickname just over a month into his term. After Newsom made a high-profile announcement in his State of the State Address about scaling back the high-speed rail project, and then backtracked, the paper dubbed him "Gov. gaslight." The editorial provided a definition of "gaslighting" so that no one would miss the point: "a tactic in which a person or entity, in order to gain more power, makes a victim question their reality," with signs including "[l]ying and denying what's been said, even in the face of clear evidence," "[s] aying one thing while actually doing another," "[u]sing confusion as a tool to manipulate perception," and "[a]ccusing everyone else of lying."

In the same vein, Newsom was quick to take credit for others' achievements if it meant claiming a headline. The NCAA bill featured in the animation—which was good legislation that I supported—had very little to do with Newsom. It was an idea that Democrat Senator Nancy Skinner made happen through tireless effort. All Newsom did was sign the bill, and it wasn't even clear until the last moment that he would do that. Yet in the animation, we see Newsom himself heroically take out the NCAA head honcho. In real life, his approval of the legislation was "orchestrated to attract national buzz," as CalMatters described it, with Newsom signing the bill on an HBO show alongside LeBron James. He was rewarded when James tweeted, "You the man Governor Gav!"

These news reports reflect an impression shared by lawmakers on both sides of the aisle after Newsom's first year: His main constituency was not the 40 million Californians he was entrusted to lead, but a national press corps he hoped would introduce him to a broader audience. The endgame was no mystery. Capitol insiders believed Newsom's habit of overhyping announcements "was motivated by an unspoken desire to pad the governor's resume for a future presidential campaign." USA Today reported that "[m]any California political observers consider Newsom's presidential ambition to be one of the state's worst-kept secrets." The Governor had a bust of John F. Kennedy sitting on his desk.

In order to "foster a national profile," Newsom repeatedly used the Mario Kart tactic, poking sticks in the eye of the President and offering himself as a virtuous alternative. The San Francisco Chronicle noted Newsom "turned his attention frequently to the national stage, charging into battle against President Trump." While he was certainly not alone in doing so, he stood out for the "countless times" in his first year that he "used his platform to criticize or make fun of" the President—in contrast to Jerry Brown, who "engaged in fewer of the political tit-for-tats that Newsom seems to relish." More broadly, the Governor went out of his way to fan partisan flames, as reflected in the Mario Kart animation's Manichean division between "red" and "blue" characters.

Yet, as USA Today noted in its end-of-year interview with Newsom, "Leading th[e] resistance has been time consuming." And California's own problems were growing.

While Rome Burned

In its December 2019 story, USA Today noted there was an impression that "the governor's first year in office has been diluted by" his attention to national politics, "resulting in a lack of progress on huge issues—a mushrooming homeless population, astronomical housing prices, a dangerous electrical grid—that have led pundits to write eulogies for the age-old California dream."

Newsom himself appeared to recognize he lacked tangible achievements, telling the Associated Press, "I think it's a mistake to look to the first year and draw a lot of big conclusions." Yet his failure to acknowledge, much less address, the state's deteriorating conditions was conspicuously at odds with his rhetoric. USA Today summarized the disconnect, noting that while Newsom had "campaigned on the enduring attraction of the mythic and potent California dream... that postcard image has taken a hit." The article pointed to "soaring" homelessness, the appearance of apps "to track human waste on sidewalks" in San Francisco, housing costs double the national average, and twice as many people leaving the state as just two years earlier, concluding: "To Newsom's constituents, taking on Trump is one task. Governing the state is another altogether."

Despite promising a "Marshall Plan" to address the housing crisis, the LA Times noted that "at the end of his first year, there are few signs the state is making the progress Newsom had promised." While he'd pledged to give homelessness "greater attention" with the creation of a "Cabinet-level homelessness czar," that position "never materialized," according to the San Francisco Chronicle. Meanwhile, 1,039 homeless died on the streets of Los Angeles County. Only after polling showed homelessness to be far and away the highest concern of voters did Newsom take the extraordinary step of devoting his entire 2020 State of the State Address to the topic.

The list goes on. Schools continued to fail, with math and reading scores declining. Nothing was done about the state's unstable tax structure or unsustainable liabilities. And Californians experienced a dystopian mix of catastrophic wildfires and frequent power outages. As to the latter, Newsom went "along with the plans of PG&E and Edison for those outages," until they were actually carried out, when he pronounced them 'intolerable.'" This, Thomas Elias wrote in the Los Angeles Daily News, "established him as even more of a utility company ally."

Despite this alliance with the utilities, Newsom sought to get in front of the public's anger by lambasting PG&E for "corporate greed" and "dog-eat-dog capitalism." But he was compromised by the extraordinary amount of funding he had taken from PG&E specifically. The Washington Post reported that "over the past two decades, Newsom and his wife have accepted more than $700,000" from PG&E, its employees, and its foundation. The Post described how PG&E guided Newsom's rise to power in San Francisco, quoting a former County Supervisor: "You couldn't be mayor in San Francisco without having the backing of PG&E. They were like the anchor, the one percent—the rich and powerful that determine the outcome of elections."

Altogether, PG&E spent $5.3 million on campaigns in 2017 and

2018, "with Newsom receiving more of that money than any other single candidate." Jerry Brown, by contrast, returned contributions from PG&E after the utility was convicted of several felonies. Personally, I have not kept any contributions from PG&E, and in 2020, I introduced legislation to prohibit PG&E from making contributions at all, since a utility is a quasi-public entity. The bill was co-authored by Democrat Legislator Kansan Chu of San Jose, but the Assembly Elections Committee Chair, a Newsom ally, refused to give it a hearing.

These issues—homelessness, housing, education, wildfires, blackouts, and the long-term sustainability of California itself—did not appear on the Mario Kart racetrack. The image of Nero fiddling while Rome burns comes to mind. Yet Newsom somehow saw a different Italian city: "This is Florence in its golden age," he said of California at the close of 2019.

A Taste of Autocracy

At the end of Newsom's first year, the Mayor of the Southern California City of Huntington Beach told USA Today, "Under him, we're getting a more authoritarian Sacramento." While words like authoritarian, autocrat, and dictator became synonymous with Newsom in 2020, 2019 provided more than a glimpse of what was to come. As a New York Times columnist noted, "Mr. Newsom has proved adept at garnering headlines and, even before the pandemic, favored governing by executive order."

Upon assuming office, Newsom immediately "added more than three dozen positions" to his personal staff and "increased his office's total budget to $24.5 million." Before long he started issuing unilateral orders as a favored mode of governance. The LA Times reported that "Newsom used executive authority to carry out some of his most consequential actions," including stopping "the approval of new hydraulic fracturing in the state," consolidating prescription drug purchases, and "irk[ing] Trump by pulling many of California's National Guard troops from their duties near the U.S.-Mexico border." He also received criticism for unilaterally diverting revenue from the new gas tax away from roads and towards favored transit projects. "What the hell were you thinking?" one lawmaker said of the directive, adding, "I don't normally talk like this."

Newsom's most noteworthy unilateral action was the one featured in the Mario Kart animation, where the unsuspecting President is pelted with a newspaper headline reading "Death Penalty Ends in California." Jerry Brown also opposed the death penalty, but recognized he had no power to abolish it. Just two years before Newsom was elected, voters had approved an initiative to keep capital punishment. During his campaign, Newsom promised he would "respect the will of the electorate" on the issue. Yet on March 12, 2019, he announced he was granting a reprieve to all 737 prisoners on death row. Although this had little practical effect—California hadn't executed anyone since 2006—the announcement "was well orchestrated for maximum media attention, including videos posted on Twitter and photos of San Quentin's capital punishment chamber being dismantled," Dan Walters wrote in CalMatters. Walters added Newsom again showed his fondness for making "grandiloquent, headline-grabbing gestures couched in moralistic terms."

Newsom evinced this same tendency to ignore legal constraints for the sake of publicity when he signed a bill to deny presidential candidates a spot on California's ballot unless they release their tax returns. The measure was plainly unconstitutional, a reason cited by Jerry Brown for vetoing the same proposal two years earlier. Yet on July 30, 2019, Newsom signed it, proclaiming in a press release that it was a "moral duty." Within months, the California Supreme Court unanimously struck the law down. Chief Justice Tani Cantil-Sakauye wrote that the Constitution is clear "it is the voters who must decide" whether a presidential candidate's refusal "to make such information available to the public will have consequences at the ballot box." In a telling moment at oral argument in the case, she had said, "We've searched the record to determine whether or not the California Legislature even considered the California Constitution in the drafting of SB 27. We didn't find anything."

* * *

Gavin Newsom's first year began with an unremarkable Inaugural Address. I watched the January 7, 2019 speech from inside a tent next to the Capitol, where the inauguration was held because of rain. The most memorable part was that the new Governor's adorable three-year-old son kept running up on the stage, interrupting his father's speech. But the LA Times revealed this was scripted, with Newsom's prepared remarks annotating after one line: "[Newsom's reference to his son Dutch, who was running around the stage]."

Newsom made an attempt at alliteration in the speech: "Our government will be progressive, principled and always on the side of the people." But by the end of that first year, it was hard to find much in his record reflecting progress or principle. It was harder still to defend the last descriptor, as never before had the chasm between our government and the people been wider. Never in recent memory had the grip of Special Interests on a California governor been more ironclad.

Even apart from the singular role of PG&E in Newsom's rise, subservience to powerful Special Interests is more than anything what defined his first year as Governor. While not depicted in the Mario animation, these interests and their lobbyists are unmistakably fueling the kart, controlling the gas and brakes, and effectively turning the wheel. As Newsom's first year drew to a close, his eagerness to please them at all costs would lead to the most destructive action by an American governor in a very long time.

CHAPTER TWO

California's Cruelest Law

"I am a 61-year-old cancer survivor. AB 5 destroyed my life, taking my over-the-phone interpreter job. Who will hire a sick senior like me? I was making good money, taking my breaks when I feel like it. During my chemotherapy this job was my salvation against depression. It made me feel useful, helping people in hospitals, pharmacies, hotels, rental companies, immigration agencies, and much more. When I was interpreting, I didn't even think about any bad things happening in my life. Since January I live with depression. Some days I don't have strength to get up in the morning, I just crawl and cry—because for eight years I've been waking up to log in and start to work. Sometimes I wish I could die. My name is Monica, and this is my AB 5 story."

In an alternate universe where 2020 never happened, Gavin Newsom might not be facing a viable recall. But he would still have earned his place in the pantheon of California's most corrupt governors by virtue of signing, celebrating, and ruthlessly enforcing the most corrupt law in our state's history.

Newsom's own former deputy chief of staff Yoshar Ali called it "one of the most destructive pieces of legislation in the past 20 years," adding, "It's truly horrific how many people are negatively impacted by it." Newsom's political godfather, Willie Brown, said the law made him want to "picket" against the "bastards" at the Capitol and the special interests that "took advantage" of them. Andrew Cuomo rejected a similar law in New York, saying he didn't want to "make the same mistake" as California. The liberal Daily Kos likewise warned other states, "Don't make the mistake California's Gavin Newsom did," with the site's founder calling the law "disastrous" and "asinine" and its supporters "shameful."

The NAACP assailed it as a "terrible law" and a "gut punch to our community." The CEO of the Black Chamber of Commerce called it a "catastrophe" responsible for "enabling, defending, and propagating systemic racism." Two hundred Ph.D. economists, including a Nobel Laureate, reported the law is "doing substantial, and avoidable, harm to the very people who now have the fewest resources and the worst alternatives available to them." One commentator called it "the most malicious and harmful law ever passed in California."

* * *

As of midnight, on August 20, 2020, Uber and Lyft were set to shut down service in California entirely. Assembly Bill 5, signed by Gavin Newsom the year before, had banned the operation of these companies as we know them. The only reason this didn't happen was a judge issued a temporary emergency stay. If voters had not passed Proposition 22 in November, exempting ridesharing providers from the law, they would have been forced to leave—putting hundreds of thousands of California drivers out of work and depriving millions of Californians of their services.

Uber and Lyft drivers are just the tip of the iceberg. AB 5 effectively bans independent work of any kind—being your own boss. With a single stroke of his pen, Governor Newsom rendered countless Californians, spanning hundreds of professions, unable to earn a living in our state. These professions range from writers and musicians, to translators and interpreters, to educators and health care professionals. Even the likes of birthday magicians and mall Santas have been ensnared by the law. If you're a parent who's had difficulty hiring a tutor to assist your child with distance learning, AB 5 is probably to blame. Many national companies now explicitly disclaim on their applications that they can no longer work with California freelancers.

While authored by a legislator from San Diego, the bill was actually written by the most powerful Special Interest at the California Capitol: massive union conglomerates that have taken over what used to be genuine worker advocacy associations and turned them into profit centers. They use these profits to install politicians whose only function is to do their bidding and pass laws that increase their profits even more—and round and round we go, as ordinary Californians pay the price.

AB 5, in particular, was the biggest windfall for these Special Interests in years. The bill's purpose was to eliminate a large non-revenue-generating sector of the workforce: independent workers whose paychecks aren't subject to union dues. Lee Ohanian of the Hoover Institution called it "an enormous political payoff," as the "new law provides hundreds of thousands of new workers for union organizing efforts once these workers become formal employees rather than independent contractors." It's the same purpose behind Governor Newsom's war on charter schools, which he's targeted in a way Jerry Brown never would. Since unionization at charters is voluntary, not automatic, they provide less revenue for the California Teachers Association—the largest of the corporate-like union conglomerates whose largesse Newsom rode to office.

Just as it didn't matter to Newsom that charter schools have proven to be the best hope for many underprivileged kids, it made no difference that the vast majority of independent contractors desire that status—often because life circumstances like being a single parent or having a disability require flexibility in their work arrangements.

AB 5 Stories

The most powerful voices speaking out against AB 5 were the law's victims, countless Californians who had their careers destroyed. In early 2020, I compiled a book of their stories and gave a copy to Governor Newsom and every California Legislator. Consider just a few:

Michelle: "I am a nail technician renting space in a tiny salon in Chico. I am a Campfire survivor who lost my home and my hometown, and I lost my husband on 4/18/19 to cancer. I am my sole provider and this bill will put me out of business."

Andy: "I work with underserved artists of color. NONE of my career as an artist, technician, designer, and producer would've been possible under AB 5. Artists of color will be less able to create their own work in a field that doesn't favor them"

John: "I am a guest orchestral conductor. Because of this bill, I just lost my first scheduled job with an orchestra – $9000 that would have put a dent in my student loans, or helped pay my insurance, or paid for food and shelter is now gone – all because of AB 5."

Esther: "I help people who don't speak English communicate with medical providers. I'm a proud senior, independent and self-sufficient. AB 5 leaves me out of work, unprotected and isolated. It takes away my pride. It was passed without taking people like me into account."

Sylvia: "I'm the Director of a small nonprofit opera. We've scrambled to comply with AB 5, but it will cost $10,000. Our nonprofit doesn't have this so I'll pay. We can't sustain this and will likely go dark. I founded the company 20 years ago so this breaks my heart."

Jodie: "I worked years to gain my skill as an American Sign Language Interpreter. It was my goal since I was 9 years old. After AB 5

I lost all 3 of my agencies. The dream I worked for is lost, I can't provide for my family and thousands of CA Deaf won't be serviced."

Eddie: "I am disabled and unhirable for a regular job. Yet as an independent contractor specializing in unique things I have been able to work and survive in LA since 1983. AB 5 has me very, very worried. I literally have no clue how much longer I can survive."

Megan: "I am a nurse practitioner. AB 5 is widening the gap in healthcare as small rural practices that can only be staffed with contractors shut their doors. Setting my own schedule has allowed me to spend time with my children that I will no longer be able to."

Jean: "I've been a tech writer in the medical device industry for 15 years, for Bay Area companies. I can't afford to live in the Bay Area so I live on the central coast. I'm now unemployed thanks to AB 5. It's devastating. I have no idea how I'll stay afloat."

Daniel: "I am a chiropractor in California. I was just terminated from my wonderful independent contract, 10 hour/week job. The company cited AB 5. I've had this job for 10 years. The job allowed me flexibility to take care of my 3 special-needs kids. Now it's gone."

Connie: "Problems standing/walking limit my ability to find employment. I choose to work as an IC because it suits my life best. Now my online teaching company stopped working with CA teachers. AB 5 is taking away my choices and livelihood and I might lose everything."

Jared: "AB 5 forced me to shut down my business. I went from making $80,000/year in home services to a minimum wage employee. My family trade is gone. I've gone from working 4 days/week to spend time with my kids to not knowing if I can make ends meet working 7 days"

Julia: "Due to mental health issues, I'm unable to work in an office. Then I started freelancing – a change that allowed me to work from my own home, on my own schedule. I now for the first time feel in control of my mental health and livelihood. AB 5 threatens this."

Kathi: "I'm begging you to suspend AB 5. I'm a 71-year-old transcriber. I raised 6 kids and went to work in my 40's but I had to retire at 62 due to health issues. I depend on my at-home transcription pay to survive and pay my bills. For 8 years I did ok, until AB 5."

Willow: "I'm an independent micro-budget producer. AB 5 shut down my series I'd planned to film in Sonoma, and I've had to rethink films, audio dramas, comic books, motion comics. People I'd planned to pay now get nothing. Congrats, you've obliterated indie film in CA."

Barbara: "I'm a proofreader. Competition is fierce and it's hard to get clients, but I did it. I was thrilled to choose jobs I was best suited for and to work when I wanted. After AB 5, Californians need not apply. Thanks Mr. Newsom for destroying my hard-earned career."

Lynn: "The ability to work independently provides me as a single mother of multiple children with special needs flexibility to earn livable wages. I CHOOSE to work independently. AB 5 does not protect the working middle class. It severely cripples it!"

These voices came from every walk of life and an astounding diversity of professions. Yet after being targeted by our state government, they quickly coalesced into a powerful movement the likes of which California had never seen. One hub of organizing was the Freelancers Against AB 5 Facebook group, which now has over 20,000 members. A survey showed this group of opponents was mainly comprised of Democrats, even though the law was passed by a Democrat Legislature and signed by a Democrat Governor. As it turns out, decent people of all political affiliations are against cruelty and corruption.

Newsom's Silence

In the weeks leading up to COVID, it was, as one headline put it, "All-AB-5, All-the-Time" at the Capitol. I led an effort to overturn the law by introducing Assembly Bill 1928, a full repeal.

On January 29, I organized a Rally to Repeal AB 5, with hundreds of independent contractors traveling to the Capitol from all across the state. My goal was not to castigate the Governor but to appeal to his conscience. Addressing the crowd, I quoted a letter Newsom had recently written to lawmakers, describing a state where millions of people come together "in pursuit of their own version of the California Dream." I then spoke to him directly: "Governor Newsom, we are here today to tell you that this cannot be reality as long as AB 5 is on the books."

Perhaps never in our history, I said, had "a legislative enactment so shattered the lives of so many people, or so shaken the foundations of our pluralist society." I listed off a small sample of the impacted professions, saying "hardly an industry or trade is unscathed." Most devastated by AB 5, I continued, "are our most vulnerable: seniors, caregivers, students, reformed convicts, single mothers, people with disabilities or health issues or mental health needs—all of whom *rely* on independent contracting."

Newsom and other proponents had absurdly described the law as a worker protection measure, even though the vast majority of independent contractors opposed these "protections" and industries with sufficiently powerful lobbyists were exempted entirely. Addressing that pretext, I recognized that "organized labor has played a vital role in humanizing the American workplace, grounding our economic life in the values of dignity, autonomy, and respect for our common humanity." But, I continued, "Assembly Bill 5 is an affront to those values, through and through. When you take your God-given talents, nurture them with heart and soul, and offer them to the world, that's not exploitation. That's self-actualization."

To conclude, I again appealed directly to the Governor. "Governor Newsom, if you are listening—you will have to realize what a failure of leadership AB 5 was. But you should also realize what a display of statesmanship it would be to now accept responsibility and correct course. Just look to the ultimate statesman, whose portrait graces our Assembly Chamber. Abraham Lincoln said, 'I shall try to correct errors when shown to be errors; and I shall adopt new views so fast as they shall appear to be true views.'"

After the rally, many of the law's victims who had come from all around the state stayed for a meeting in the Governor's Office. I had asked Newsom to meet with them, but he refused, instead delegating the task to his Legislative Affairs Secretary. Then this staffer cancelled at the last moment—claiming he was "with the Governor"—and the group was left to talk to three low-level staff members who did not even seem to have titles.

Over the next month, as I prepared to bring my repeal measure to the Assembly Floor for a vote, I continued to focus my attempts at persuasion on the Governor. If he came out for repeal the Legislature would almost certainly pass it. I pointed out that his State of the State Address in February would be a "perfect opportunity to show the leadership Californians are looking for and call off the disastrous" law. I predicted that whether he supported the repeal "could define the rest of his governorship." After the State of the State, I acknowledged that Newsom's "failure to address the fallout from AB 5 was jarring," but I said "he can still provide the leadership this moment demands by supporting" the repeal vote.

Meanwhile, the Special Interests behind AB 5 organized a "lobby day" at the Capitol. It is rather unusual to have a lobby day for a bill that has already passed. They were making it clear to legislators, and presumably Newsom, that there would be consequences for not toeing their line. When I asked one legislator to support the repeal, he literally shuddered and said, "I'll get my throat slit."

Without support from the Governor, the repeal vote failed on February 28. As I had said at the rally, that's what happens when humanist values give way to brute political force.

Newsom's Denialism

For seven months, Newsom never addressed the devastation caused by AB 5. At one live video event on Twitter, he asked people to tweet him their questions. Dozens asked about AB 5, far more than any other topic. He ignored all of them.

Finally, on April 24, well into the COVID era, Newsom was asked at a press conference about all the jobs that had been lost because of the law. He responded with one of the most stunning statements in California political history. Even though the fallout from the bill was one of the biggest stories in California for months—and even though I'd placed a book of hundreds of heartbreaking stories on his desk—he answered simply: "Respectfully, I'm not sure those jobs were killed."

It's worth noting who the question came from. A reporter for *LA Blade*, an LGBT magazine, asked specifically about the law's harsh impacts on the LGBT community. Newsom, of course, had risen to prominence as an advocate for same-sex marriage. Yet here he was, silencing the voices of LGBT Californians, erasing their suffering. Later, when Newsom lauded a Supreme Court decision on LGBT workplace protections, I reminded him of this denialism: "When LA Blade told him about a loss of work in the LGBT community from AB 5, he dismissed their plight. For this Governor, social justice ends where the influence of special interests begins."

To enact a harmful policy is a mistake of judgment, and redeemable. But to pretend the people you've harmed don't exist is a matter of character and fitness to lead. After months of appealing to the Governor's conscience, this was a moment where I began to think there was truly no point to it. In frustration, I tweeted, "'Respectfully, I'm not sure those jobs were killed' could be the first line of Gavin

Newsom's political obituary." He has of course added many more lines since.

* * *

To this day Newsom has never once so much as acknowledged any of AB 5's many victims, with a single exception: Willie Brown, the former San Francisco Mayor and self-described "Ayatollah of the Assembly" who had given Newsom his political start.

In September, Politico reported that Brown lost his popular column for the San Francisco Chronicle, making him the "latest ensnared by California's new gig-economy law limiting freelancers"—that is, "until onetime protege Gov. Gavin Newsom signed a bill." The Politico story continued: "Earlier in the day, some of Brown's powerful friends in politics contacted Newsom in an effort to get him to move quickly on the bill to get Brown's Sunday column back in the paper as soon as possible."

After Newsom complied, creating this "Willie Brown Exception," he texted his former mentor: "I signed the bill, write the damn column!"

* * *

The tragic human costs of AB 5 were heightened by Newsom's COVID-19 lockdowns. This was part and parcel of the corruption, to be discussed in Chapter 6, that defined California's COVID response. But one recent detail is worth noting here.

In August, we learned about a sordid scandal connected with AB 5's passage. One of the Capitol's most powerful legislators had an extended affair with a homeless domestic worker, which he began by impersonating (of all people) another legislator on the "What's Your Price?" dating site. This same woman had testified before the Assembly

Labor Committee as a witness in favor of AB 5, claiming the bill would help workers like her. At the time, her affair with the lawmaker, who coauthored the law, had been going on for years.

She had now gone on the record saying she was "exploited" by the lawmaker as well as by the California Labor Federation and other Special Interests to advance the bill. Here's what she said in her own words, a quote that should be inscribed on the dome of our State Capitol: "These unions controlled my testimonies, got stories out of me, and then tossed me out. It was a payday for them, not to help domestic workers." She added she had "never experienced abuse on this level" and was used as a "prop" to bolster AB 5.

Having at that point spent two years fighting against AB 5, it came as no surprise to me that the same interest groups that abuse workers collectively through legislation also abuse workers individually through the process of getting bills enacted. They'll do whatever it takes to push their agenda. And many California politicians are only too willing to go along, no matter who gets hurt, and no matter that it's ruining our state. When the story about the secret affair broke, it only served to confirm the larger scandal that's played out in plain sight: Special Interests hijacking our government and running roughshod over anyone who gets in the way.

* * *

Gavin Newsom held the job of lieutenant governor, with essentially no responsibilities, for eight years. He had all the time in the world to think about what he might do if he became governor. He came into office with the backwinds of a strong national economy. There was no virus in sight. He could have used his political capital as a first-year governor to tackle our state's intractable problems. If he wasn't willing to do that, he could at least have pursued an agenda embodying some kind of vision or values.

Instead, he used one of the highest and most influential offices there is, what he's called "the best job in the world," to play a shallow and soulless game. He maneuvered to enrich Special Interest groups in every way he could. He knowingly inflicted searing harm on the most vulnerable in our society and compounded our state's fundamental challenges. That was the prelude to COVID-19.

CHAPTER THREE

COVID Begins

"We project that roughly 56 percent of our population—25.5 million people—will be infected with the virus over an eight week period."
– Gavin Newsom, March 18, 2020

Gavin Newsom has been credited with responding quickly to COVID-19. Where it is deserved, I have given him credit myself. In the early days, I went out of my way to be as glowing as possible in the name of a unified and non-politicized state response.

Newsom's overall promptness, however, is largely a myth. For one thing, California had been de-prioritizing pandemic preparedness for years and that continued with Newsom's first two budgets. More to the point, as I will discuss in Chapter 11, nearly every facet of California's public health response unrelated to restricting human activity—building healthcare capacity, ramping up testing supplies, expanding testing locations, cutting red tape, developing contact tracing—was lagging to the point of neglect.

Even the notion that Newsom provided timely public health guidance is exaggerated. As late as March 10, 2020, six days after Newsom declared the COVID-19 State of Emergency, his Department of Public Health put out a notice that it was "not recommending the cancellation of public events," stating that "the health risk from COVID-19 to the general public remains low at this time." And his most celebrated action, issuing the "first" statewide state-at-home order, actually followed in the wake of six Bay Area counties that were the first in the nation do so.

Newsom's State of the State Address, delivered on February 19, did not mention the novel coronavirus once, even amid growing recognition that this was not going to be just China's problem. I remember this well, as I sat next to a Senator on the Health Committee during the State of the State and quizzed him extensively on what was being done. Throughout February, Newsom's very active Twitter feed was devoted mostly to attacking the President, only mentioning COVID-19 once before the end of the month, and only then for the purpose of virtue-signaling ("DON'T be racist."). His third COVID-related tweet, on March 3, was to complain about Amazon's "absurd" price for hand sanitizers.

Once the virus did become his focus, Newsom made bewildering statements that flew in the face of the evidence—something Californians would become familiar with in the ensuing months. On March 18, the day before issuing the original stay-at-home order, Newsom wrote a one-page letter to President Trump with an extraordinary prediction: "We project that roughly 56 percent of our population—25.5 million people—will be infected with the virus over an eight week period." This confident assertion, made without qualification or caveat, came with no evidence (and bad arithmetic: 25.5 million people was roughly 65 percent of the population, not 56 percent). In fact, at the time experts lacked "the data to make reliable predictions." Stanford epidemiologist John Ioannidis said, "Right now, we are not using science. We are just using fear, panic, anecdotal reports." Dr. Mark Ghaly, Newsom's Health and Human Services Secretary, quickly walked back the Governor's wild claim, but it had already been widely disseminated to the public.

By this point, the Legislature had recessed and would not return for seven weeks. Newsom was giving daily press conferences and issuing Executive Orders in bunches. The economy was shut down.

The concept of an "essential" industry had been invented. Forty million Californians were stuck at home, but willing to do their part. The COVID era had begun.

* * *

I do not doubt that Gavin Newsom took steps early in the pandemic that he believed would advance public health and protect Californians from the virus. But it soon became clear this was not his only goal. After a year of trying desperately, and mostly failing, to thrust himself into the spotlight, suddenly COVID-19 offered a ready-made opportunity to become a national figure. This was an opportunity he did not intend to waste.

PART II

AMERICA'S WORST COVID RESPONSE

CHAPTER FOUR

Self-Promotional

"#PresidentNewsom" – hashtag briefly trending on Twitter on April 8, 2020

In the early stages of COVID-19, Gavin Newsom's press conferences were must-see TV. Or at least he imagined them to be. Official social media posts would breathlessly advertise his briefings, with liberal use of all caps ("TUNE IN"). To build anticipation, his media advisories would tease a "major announcement," such as when the initial stay-at-home order came down.

And Newsom was indeed getting a lot of Californians to tune in. After all, he literally had a captive audience and was telling people what daily activities were no longer allowed, something of inherent interest to the public. Newsom's pressers in March garnered hundreds of thousands of views on social media, in addition to everyone watching or listening on TV or radio. Personally, I watched them closely at the time; nowadays, most of the public has tuned them out and I just read summaries. Our trial against Newsom on October 21 was watched on Facebook by several times more people than watched the Governor's press conference that day.

Newsom also became "a fixture on cable TV," hitting the daytime and late-night talk show circuit. David McCuan, a veteran California political analyst, said that in the early months of 2020 Newsom was "interested in being on national network shows, on having a national profile, on building that sizzle.'' He appeared on the Daily Show, the View, the Ellen Show, ExtraTV, TODAY, Late Night with Seth Meyers, the View (again), and Late Night with James Corden. Meyers mentioned on the air that when he asked Newsom to appear on the show, "you said yes right away." The Governor could hardly contain his delight in getting to partner with celebrities like Shaquille O'Neil, Kim Kardashian, and Larry David on Public Service Announcements (full disclosure: I enjoyed the David clip). On Late Night with Seth Meyers, he giddily explained how he got in touch with Shaq through "a friend of a friend." "It makes me feel good about our celebrities in the State of California," Newsom said.

But it wasn't all fun and games. During the Seth Meyers appearance, Newsom described COVID-19 as an existential threat to the entire state that only he could defeat. "I'm trying to save 40 million Californians," he said.

A Viral Campaign

Newsom should not be blamed for going on television to educate the public about a novel virus. But it soon became clear that getting publicity was an end in itself that was undermining California's COVID response.

In an April 29 story headlined, "Criticism grows over Gov. Gavin Newsom's management of the coronavirus crisis," the Los Angeles Times noted that "Newsom has revealed new policy initiatives at almost all of his daily news conferences." This "quick pace," the article said, "has led to premature introductions of some of his plans." For instance, on April 22, Newsom had announced California would begin to "pull back and lean in" (however that's possible) to resume elective surgeries. In fact, surgeries could not yet resume, as new guidelines did not exist and wouldn't be issued for several days. This created frustration among hospitals over Newsom's "mixed message," according to the California Hospital Association's president, Carmela Coyle. When new guidelines appeared the following week, Coyle acknowledged they'd had to be developed "rapidly" because of the Governor's hasty announcement.

In another splashy announcement, Newsom unveiled a "Californians for All" volunteering initiative. CalNonprofits, VolunteerMatch, and CalVolunteers, representing nearly 10,000 charitable organizations in California, had all offered to partner with the Administration and "suggested a better way to roll out the initiative," but their "advice was ignored." The Director of CalNonprofits said, "The fact is that we in the nonprofit community know how to recruit volunteers, so why not ask us? Why not use the mechanisms that are in place to already do that?" She answered her own question: "They were in a hurry to do something, and it doesn't seem that they gave it the thought that a project like that needs." The LA Times noted that a week after Newsom unveiled the initiative, "the state changed course and is now working with VolunteerMatch."

At another press conference, the Governor made news when he "touted an executive order" on scope-of-practice reforms for nurse practitioners. But, the Times reported, "it was unclear precisely what the order would do, and it did not take effect immediately." It wasn't until two weeks later that any actual policy affecting nurse practitioners materialized, "without the scope of practice changes advocates had expected." Similarly, the Associated Press reported that Newsom's "initial claims on plans to house the homeless...haven't matched reality." Newsom not only quietly revised a promise of 51,000 hotel rooms down to 15,000, but falsely claimed the state was "in real time, quite literally" negotiating with hotels when counties did the negotiating. The head of the California Hotel and Lodging Association said he wanted to help but "the ground keeps shifting under us and the priorities change on a regular basis."

In the early days, I gave Newsom the benefit of the doubt. But as these episodes piled up, the pattern became clear. The mistakes were not an inevitable byproduct of urgent actions. They were an avoidable consequence of urgent announcements. Newsom was offering the media something new every day to keep himself front and center in the news cycle. It was a strategy entirely extraneous to—in fact, at odds with—what would help the state respond to COVID-19. Newsom's performance began to feel less like a coordinated pandemic response and more like a political campaign, with a different plank of the Governor's "platform" released each day.

An April 19 column in the New York Times—a paper Newsom would cater to with the first question at press conferences—noted that Newson's "youthful face and bold pronouncements have become a familiar feature on national television." But, the piece continued, in his "flurry of recent news releases, details have been fuzzy and substance often fallen short of hype," citing examples like an overhyped eviction moratorium and a "heralded" school district agreement that didn't do what he claimed. The Times column concluded that while Newsom had "delivered fanfare," if he didn't "follow through" his "national stature" would be "fleeting."

One consequence of Newsom's rush to make news was he had little use for the Legislature. "The problem that my members have is the lack of lead time," Democrat Speaker of the Assembly, Anthony Rendon, said in late April. "They feel like they are being told just before the public is told, but without enough time to provide any meaningful feedback." After one major announcement, Democrat Assemblyman Phil Ting of San Francisco said it "would be great to get a heads-up directly from the governor's office rather than watching it on national TV." I raised similar concerns repeatedly. Yet Newsom dismissed all of us with what the Los Angeles Times called a "familiar defense," saying, "Some are consumed by process, personality, intrigue, who's up, who's down? We are for actually solving a major, major problem." He also suggested that he couldn't let collaboration with the Legislature keep him away from the cameras, saying on April 21, "I recognize my unique responsibility to them but also to you members of the press."

In Cuomo's Shadow

Even as he reveled in this newfound attention, something was rankling Newsom. Another governor across the country was getting much more of it. While Newsom had a California audience for his press conferences, Andrew Cuomo's routinely got carried live on CNN and other national networks. (Cuomo was recently awarded an Emmy for these performances.) With the Democratic Presidential Primary in disarray, some were even suggesting Cuomo ride in as a White Knight.

The rivalry between Newsom and Cuomo was not subtle. A March 27 LA Times story described the two as "well-known Democrats with presidential ambitions who could someday face each other as rivals." As Newsom wore out the phrase "meet this moment"—using it up to 20 times in the same press conference—one could sense he feared he was missing his own moment, with Cuomo continuing to overshadow him. An article in the New York Times noted, "While Mr. Newsom has emulated his New York counterpart with daily #Newsomatnoon briefings," he "has yet to achieve the authenticity and gravitas that has earned Mr. Cuomo a cultlike following."

The Newsom operation tried in vain to seed a counter-narrative: California had fewer COVID cases at the time than New York, so why was Cuomo getting all the attention? In one self-congratulatory statement, Newsom's spokesman proclaimed that "Gov. Newsom has moved swiftly to protect human life, and he has taken aggressive and urgent actions to help Californians get through these challenging times. Because of those efforts and the actions of millions of Californians who are staying home, California has both flattened the curve and helped millions of its most vulnerable residents."

Newsom's attempts to claim the spotlight became increasingly desperate, as his tendency to make premature announcements graduated to a penchant for outright fabrications. On April 30, the Sacramento Bee published a scathing editorial headlined "Gavin Newsom's half-baked announcements harm credibility, raise troubling questions." The Editorial Board revived its "Gov. Gaslight" moniker as it blasted Newsom for a press conference he held with the owner of the Sacramento Kings outside the team's old arena, which was to be converted to a COVID treatment facility. Newsom had praised the Kings' "philanthropy," suggesting he had procured the facility at no cost. But the Bee later discovered it was actually costing taxpayers $1.5 for three months. The editorial invoked Churchill's aphorism that a "a lie gets halfway around the world before the truth has a chance to get its pants on."

The Bee also cited Newsom's "dramatic" March 23 announcement that "Tesla founder Elon Musk was donating over 1,000 ventilators to California." As it turned out, the Bee reported, "not a single unit was ever actually delivered to hospitals." Because Newsom so often "hurried to get in front of the TV cameras without worrying about the details," he was giving "reporters a reason to be much more skeptical of what he says." By December, the Bee was still referring to Newsom's "weakness for flashy press announcements that later turn out to be flimsy on substance."

Newsom even managed to offend Capitol reporters, when he thanked them "for staying on message." That's "not exactly how we'd put it, I think" quipped Jeremy White of Politico. Dan Walters, a respected reporter of 60 years, said the comment "implies that our job is to help Newsom peddle his message." He called it "insulting" and said Newsom "owes our profession an apology." For a Governor who had consolidated so much power, any suggestion of conscripting the press into his service was alarming. Added Walters: "in the political world 'on message' has a very specific meaning."

The President of California

Despite all of these machinations, Newsom's national presence was still a small shadow of Cuomo's. In an April 2 Los Angeles Times column, "Dean of the Capitol" George Skelton wrote that "Andrew Cuomo has been drawing lots of speculation about maybe becoming an upgraded Democratic presidential nominee, pushing aside bland Joe Biden. But there hasn't been a peep about California Gov. Gavin Newsom." So Newsom tried playing another card: perhaps he could assume the status of something more than a governor by making California something more than a state. On April 9 a Bloomberg News headline read, "Gavin Newsom Declares California a 'Nation State.'" Surely Cuomo couldn't compete with *that.*

One supportive column actually likened Newsom's declaration to the outbreak of the Civil War at Fort Sumter and the Civil-Rights-era defiance of Little Rock and Montgomery. "There is no reason that states can't adopt a racist playbook for other ends," the columnist reasoned. Newsom himself explained the term as a reference not just to California's "scale and scope," but to a "narrative of punching above our weight." Now, I cherish our state's uniqueness as much as anyone. But California's large size doesn't make us a Nation State, any more than Jupiter's makes it a solar system. We can take pride in being Californians without diminishing our place as Americans. It is our leading role in *advancing* American ideals, not setting ourselves apart from them, that gives California its singular place in U.S. history.

Newsom used the term Nation State sporadically in March, but it truly made its debut on April 7 in a national TV appearance. That night, Newsom put all of his chips on the table, hoping for a breakthrough moment where he would enter the American consciousness in the way Governor Cuomo had. In an extraordinary three-minute segment on the Rachel Maddow Show, "Newsom's political career peaked," Gil Duran would write. Then, the dust settled to reveal one of the biggest scandals in California history.

* * *

The Maddow appearance took place during MSNBC's 6 PM hour the night of April 7. Newsom came on the air towards the beginning of the show. After briefly describing California's touch-and-go PPE acquisition efforts, Newsom proceeds with an air of high drama.

"We're not waiting around any longer," he says. "In the last 48 hours we have secured through a consortia of non-profits and a manufacturer here in the state of California, upwards of 200 million masks, on a monthly basis, that we're confident we can supply the needs of the state of California, potentially the needs of other western states." Newsom continues, "We decided, enough's enough, let's use the purchasing power of the state of California as a Nation State." Moments later he reiterates, "We decided, enough of the small ball, let's use our purchasing power."

The following morning, one could almost hear the sound of champagne corks popping in the Governor's Office. #PresidentNewsom had started trending on Twitter.

* * *

In peeling back the layers of the BYD China scandal, it is hard to know where to start. Perhaps the best place is with the fact that Rachel Maddow caught Newsom lying in the moment.

Thirty-four seconds into the appearance, Newsom announces he's secured the 200 million masks through a "manufacturer here in the State of California." A surprised Maddow interpreted this claim the way Newsom hoped viewers would: "Those masks will be manufactured in California?" Newsom, clearly rattled, concedes: "No they'll be manufactured overseas but we were able to source them through a California manufacturer." What Newsom meant is that the Chinese company he signed the contract with, BYD (short for "Build Your Dreams), has a California affiliate with a lobbyist in Sacramento. The head of that subsidiary, incidentally, contributed $40,000 to Newsom's campaign for Governor. When Newsom mentions the manufacturer of the masks a third time in the interview, he still carefully avoids saying *China*, stammering as he alludes to "a large manufacturer with appropriate contacts in Asia."

Maddow's other on-air comments are also revealing. Twice in this brief segment she mentions the newsworthiness of the deal. "You are making significant news here Governor," she reassures him, to which Newsom gratefully nods and says "yeah." She later says, "I think you are going to make national news with this." Newsom's team had clearly gone to great lengths to convince Maddow to have him on the show because this had the potential to be a national news story.

It would soon become obvious that getting the TV segment and generating that national story was the main impetus for the deal, and there's a hint of this in Newsom's on-air comments as well. After announcing 200 million masks would be coming in and California could even become a PPE exporter, Newsom reports that "we just inked a number of contracts in the last few days that give me confidence in being able to say that." What we would later learn is that other deals for a similar volume of masks were reached and jettisoned. Newsom wired $457 million to "Blue Flame," a company started by a pair of political operatives just three days earlier. A CalMatters investigation uncovered that the state had to claw back the money when bankers flagged the transaction as "suspicious." A $800 million contract with a company started up by a retired politician and represented by a top Sacramento lobbyist was also cancelled, though the timing is less clear. Finally, the $1 billion no-bid deal with BYD China—with half of the money paid upfront, something unheard of in state contracting—provided Newsom with the "confidence to be able to say" what he did on the Maddow show.

I learned about the BYD deal when California journalists picked it up. I was not alone. The Sacramento Bee reported, "Newsom made national headlines when he announced the plan on The Rachel Maddow Show last week. He also surprised his counterparts in the Legislature, most of whom learned of the deal from MSNBC"—even though he was supposedly acting pursuant to spending authority we as a Legislature had granted him. As Miriam Pawel reported in the New York Times: "Lawmakers, informed only minutes before Mr. Newsom's announcement on national TV, were told emergency approval was essential because a $495 million check had to be cut within 48 hours. They were not given copies of contracts, details about costs and quality controls or plans to distribute and allocate the protective gear."

As we learned incredible details about the deal in the days and weeks that followed, Newsom still refused to answer questions about it. BYD was actually an electric vehicle manufacturer and had only two months earlier started making masks in Shenzhen. An LA Times investigation had found the company's buses had "mechanical and performance issues" among other quality problems. The City of Albuquerque sued BYD because its $133 million in buses were "riddled with defects," including "batteries that could go up in flames 'with little possibility of putting out the fire.'"

Congress had banned BYD from receiving federal contracts because of national security concerns that the company would spy on Americans. When Democrat Congressman John Garamendi, who drafted the federal ban, learned BYD was making masks he exclaimed, "What the hell? What is our government doing? They may very well flood the market with substandard devices." He added, "We believe BYD is controlled by the Chinese government and quite probably by the People's Liberation Army."

An exposé by *Vice News*, published four days after Newsom's Maddow appearance, highlighted not only the company's control by the Chinese government and history of defective products, but also "ties to forced labor" and fines for not paying minimum wage to Chinese workers at its California electronics plant. In explaining how BYD had "no history of making personal protective equipment, and yet days after the FDA approval, it secured a $1 billion deal to supply masks to California," *Vice* cited an LA Times investigation describing BYD as a "skilled political operator." That investigation found that the "company's business model involves hiring lobbyists and grant writers to secure no-bid purchases by public agencies, and it has invited public officials on foreign junkets and employed their close associates." The company's Sacramento lobbyist, Mark Weideman, also represented two other companies to which Newsom had awarded COVID-related contracts. After the *Vice* exposé, BYD filed a defamation lawsuit but only took issue with two specific claims.

In light of all of this, I along with many lawmakers on both sides of the aisle raised urgent questions about quality, timely delivery, and other concerns. We repeatedly asked to see the contract and were rebuffed. "I care about producing a big result," Newsom condescendingly said. "Others again are going to consume themselves around process. We're going to consume ourselves around saving lives." The Los Angeles Times—apparently also consumed by "process" and not "saving lives" and other "big results" like Newsom was—submitted a public records request to obtain the contract. Newsom absurdly denied it on the basis of "attorney-client privilege." A Senate hearing lasted four hours yet "yielded only generalities and evasive responses from Newsom administration officials." Newsom's only given reason for continuing to hide the contract—that disclosure would "imperil delivery"—implied he was afraid BYD would break the deal even though he'd already paid the company $495 million. Observing that Newsom had "blatantly stonewalled," the Sacramento Bee editorialized that "the administration's shifting excuses for hiding the contract don't add up." It was a month before Newsom finally relented and released it.

The revelations kept getting worse. We learned Newsom had paid BYD $3.30 per mask, while Los Angeles Mayor Eric Garcetti paid Honeywell $0.79 per mask. An expert with Raymond Associates told the LA Times that at the time Newsom made the deal, California could have made large quantities of masks for "easily under a dollar," adding that the state "could have propped up its own factories and employed Californians out of work." While Newsom had confidently said on Maddow that the PPE would be in California in "a few weeks," a month went by without any sign of the promised N-95 masks.

The deal appeared to be falling apart, and Newsom even suggested we could live without it. On May 4, our doubts were confirmed: BYD's masks had failed the required safety test by the National Institute for Occupational Safety and Health. Newsom claimed the masks had only "been delayed a little bit," so the agency clarified: "certification of the masks was denied, not delayed, contradicting comments Gov. Gavin Newsom made last week," reported the Bee. An on-site assessment found the masks "not acceptable," and a review of "the design, manufacturing and quality inspection of the device was concerning."

BYD was forced to give California a partial refund, having missed the April 30 deadline. Then, a month later on May 31, the deal officially collapsed when BYD's masks were failed for a second time by the federal regulator. At this point, the contract was null and void; the silver lining was California had gotten out of paying an inflated price and could instead pay much less to an American manufacturer. Yet inexplicably, Newsom interceded to resurrect the voided contract. While he'd acknowledged that California was overpaying—blaming the "Wild West" PPE market of early April—he declined the chance to nix the deal and put out a new bid. By the time BYD finally received approval on the third try and masks began arriving, it had been three months, not a "few weeks," since Newsom had wired the company $495 million and taken to the Rachel Maddow Show to tell the world of his heroics on behalf of the Nation State of California.

If a recall were modeled after an impeachment, the BYD affair might be the first article. On a matter of vital importance, personal protective equipment for our frontline healthcare workers, Newsom leveraged their safety to land a segment on primetime cable news. He threw around hundreds of millions of dollars without the slightest vetting so that he'd have the "confidence" to produce a moment of high-stakes political theater. He acted behind the back of the Legislature and for weeks denied any attempt at oversight of this vast expenditure of questionable legality. He misled if not outright lied to lawmakers and the public repeatedly. His overall handling of the matter showed a governor at best in over his head, and at worst unfit to lead.

* * *

It's no secret why Newsom tried so hard to use COVID-19 to build his national profile. It's the same reason he put out the inane Mario Kart video intended for national consumption. It's the same reason he spends his time trolling United States Senators and Supreme Court Justices on matters that have nothing to do with California. In an April

1 interview on CNN, Newsom said, unprompted, "I don't care who's up and down, who's polls are looking better than someone else's, or who wants to run for president or who doesn't." No one believed it. Even in the early stages of the crisis, lawmakers told me privately they could see every decision Newsom made was based on what would play best with future Iowa caucusgoers. Noting that Newsom was "touted as a future presidential candidate at the start of his term," Politico quoted veteran state political analyst David McCuan as saying he revealed a "fatal personality flaw" in trying to use the pandemic to build "sizzle."

After Kamala Harris was selected to be Joe Biden's running mate, I posted what became Politico's Tweet of the Day: "Now that Kamala Harris has elbowed Gavin Newsom out of running for president any time soon, perhaps he can give his full attention to the parochial matter of governing California." Gil Duran, the former press secretary for Jerry Brown, made a similar point. In an August 20 op-ed headlined "Coronavirus failures—and Kamala's rise—thwart Gov. Newsom's presidential dreams," Duran marked Newsom's "transition from a potential future president to a likely future has-been." He said, "Once Newsom accepts that he will never be president, he'll be free to govern California...instead of attempting to triangulate his way to 1600 Pennsylvania Ave."

Gavin Newsom is hardly the first politician, or first California Governor, to aspire to higher office. Nor is he the first to be accused of politically motivated decisions. But this was a moment of trauma and uncertainty like we had never seen. All of our lives had been upended. With so many people sacrificing so much, our Governor was cashing in that shared sacrifice for self-promotion, as California began a slow-motion descent towards the worst outcomes of the COVID era. The most troubling consequence, however, was felt almost immediately: one-man rule.

CHAPTER FIVE

Lawless

"I think Mr. Kiley's ideas work well in theory, but they don't work in practice." – Attorney for Governor Newsom, on the "idea" of checks and balances

On April 1, Gavin Newsom said he saw the coronavirus public health crisis as an "opportunity" to impose a political and ideological agenda. It wasn't a case of April Fools.

Reporter: "Do you see the potential, as some others in the party do, for a new progressive era, the opportunity for additional progressive steps because of this crisis?"

Newsom: "Yes, absolutely, we see this as an opportunity to reshape the way we do business and how we govern. There is opportunity for reimagining a progressive era as it pertains to capitalism. The answer is yes."

I was watching this press conference live and could not believe what I'd heard. What might have come across as a conspiracy theory if someone floated it on the Internet was readily acknowledged by the Governor to be his actual plan: using the State of Emergency and the emergency powers it conferred to attain political ends that could not be realized with ordinary powers in ordinary times. In the weeks and months that followed, this project of political transformation was of a piece with Newsom's overriding desire to use COVID-19 to muscle his way into the national spotlight. Both meant casting aside any legal barriers that stood in the way: checks and balances, separation of powers, and the Constitution itself.

Granted, these foundational institutions were not in good shape to start with. For years, politicians and Special Interests in Sacramento had been dismantling the architecture of self-government, brick by brick. But in 2020, the entire edifice came crashing down.

The Path of Rome

On May 8, 2020, Governor Newsom announced his 38th Executive Order of the State of Emergency, mandating universal absentee voting for the November Election. This was a brand-new policy, yet the only statutory authority the Governor cited for its promulgation—as with almost all of his other Orders to date—was a 50-year-old law known as the California Emergency Services Act. Overhauling an election six months away, Newsom claimed, was within the scope of the emergency powers conferred by the Act

A bill then making its way through the Assembly, authored by the Democrat Chair of the Elections Committee, already proposed the all-absentee policy. The reason the Governor couldn't wait for the bill became clear when he issued a press release crowing that California was the "first state in the nation" to go all-absentee. With the election still six months away, this was the real "urgency" for which emergency powers were being invoked: the race for headlines. And Newsom got what he wanted, with headlines like "California becomes first state to switch November election to all-mail voting" (Politico), "Joe Biden praises Gov. Gavin Newsom's mail-in voting order" (Deadline), and "Gov. Gavin Newsom makes California the first state to enact automatic vote-by-mail for the November 2020 election" (Vox). Other states, of course, were still functioning democracies where new laws needed to be enacted by a legislature.

At the time, I said publicly that exercising emergency powers to address a public health crisis may be necessary and appropriate, but exploiting those powers to advance a political agenda is illegal and dangerous. Indeed, by claiming a public health justification for Executive Orders that plainly lacked one, the Governor was weakening our ability to build trust for policies that were genuinely needed in relation to COVID-19 or future health threats. Yet three weeks later, the Governor issued another unilateral Executive Order making further sweeping changes to the upcoming election.

My colleague James Gallagher and I had had enough. On June 11, we walked into a nearby courthouse, and so began the case of *Gallagher and Kiley v. Newsom.*

* * *

At this point in time, we were all well-acquainted with the Newsom dictatorship. Putting aside that word's 20th-century connotations, its Roman origins relate specifically to emergencies and the absolute power the appointed individual could assume for their duration. As we would later tell the California Court of Appeal, Newsom "is no Caesar, but his legal theory in this case and ruling philosophy this year are that of *dictatorlegibus faciendis.* The Executive can make laws at will, and the participation of the Legislature is at his discretion."

On May 8, I released the first version of a document that produced a greater reaction than I was anticipating. It was a no-frills testament to the collapse of constitutional government in California, listing in a single compendium every Newsom Executive Order (then 37, now 57), along with every law he had unilaterally changed (then over 175, now over 400). In short, it laid bare the anatomy of one-man rule. While people were living every day in this world of rule-by-decree, seeing in one place the extent to which life in California had been single-handedly remade seemed to strike a chord.

All of these laws that Newsom had amended, suspended, or overhauled since declaring the State of Emergency were duly enacted through the legislative process set out in the Constitution. And each one was undone by Newsom with the stroke of a pen. But what's worse is he was also creating laws out of whole cloth, something the "Constitution expressly prohibits." While it was a public health emergency that Newsom declared, he was not sticking to the Public Health Code. The tentacles of his rule reached into 16 other codes, touching nearly every facet of our lives: Businesses & Professions, Civil Procedure, Corporations, Education, Elections, Family, Financial, Government, Harbors & Navigation, Health & Safety, Labor, Public Resources, Revenue & Taxation, Unemployment Insurance, Vehicle, and Welfare & Institutions.

Newsom had taken over the job of the Legislature—and did not deny it. To the contrary, he strenuously maintained that a State of Emergency, no matter how long it lasts, "centralizes the State's powers in the hands of the Governor." His words eerily echoed what James Madison said the U.S. Constitution was designed to prevent: "The accumulation of all powers, legislative, executive, and judiciary, in the same hands...may justly be pronounced the very definition of tyranny."

The "Second Branch"

At an April 21 press conference, Newsom was asked whether he was usurping legislative authority. In answering, he referred to the Legislature as "a second of three branches." He quickly added that we are a "co-equal branch," but that didn't rewind the Freudian slip, which was inaccurate in any case. Our State Constitution lists the Legislature first among the three branches.

After one far-reaching Executive Order, the Governor made a

comment reflecting his view of the Legislature as an essentially decorative body—akin to what the Roman Senate became in the Imperial Era or what the Duma is in present day Russia. Newsom allowed that we could, if we wanted, pass a law on the topic of the Order, but only if it was exactly the same as his edict. "We appreciate their work and, to the extent they want to codify it, I think that could help as well," Newsom said. "Why not?"

Eventually, more Members of the Legislature came to realize that by centralizing the State's powers in his hands, Newsom had not only assumed control in some general sense, but had taken over their jobs in particular. Legislators in both parties expressed alarm at the Governor's consolidation of power and he became increasingly isolated at the Capitol. The ides of May produced headlines like "Lawmakers deliver their harshest criticism of Newsom yet" (Politico), "Bipartisan lawmakers criticize Newsom's COVID-19 spending, warn of 'overreach'" (Sacramento Bee), "Time to cut off Newsom's blank check" (LA Times), and "Capitol distress over Newsom's emergency powers" (KCRA). The Associated Press would report, "Lawmakers of both political parties have criticized Newsom, a Democrat, for not sufficiently including them in his sweeping declarations and budget decisions since the pandemic began."

Kevin Mullin, who was the second highest-ranking Member of the Assembly as its Speaker pro Tempore, said in a speech on the Assembly Floor that "the Governor of this State has seemingly unlimited power to issue Executive Orders with zero warning to the legislative branch whereby the elected representatives of the people have very little oversight." Mullin noted that over a seven-week period the "Governor issued 30 Executive Orders," and "very few of those Orders with wide-ranging policy implications had any meaningful impact from this lawmaking body." Democratic Phil Ting of San Francisco, who chaired the Assembly Budget Committee, described the Governor's "huge overreach of authority" and his "disdain to properly communicate with the Legislature," observing that "[t]he governor does not have complete authority to do whatever he wants." Ting added, "What's the point of a Legislature if we're, like the public, watching TV to get information?" Senator Holly Mitchell, a Democrat from Los Angeles, would later say, "The Legislature has repeatedly called for the Executive Branch to collaborate on COVID-19 response. But time and again, the Legislature has been put in the position of simply giving a yes or no answer to the Governor's priorities." Expressing frustration over many things the Governor had not handled well with his unilateral orders, one leading Democrat Legislator said to me, "He's not a monarch!" David McCuan, a veteran California political analyst, noted Newsom had "very few friends in the legislature."

Newsom also tried to use the farcically compressed budget process to slip in a massive consolidation of executive authority that would outlive the State of Emergency. But the Legislative Analyst's Office's caught on to what he was trying to do, warning that his proposals "raise serious concerns about the Legislature's role in future decisions." Not known for its rhetorical excess, the LAO said it was "very troubled by the degree of authority that the administration is requesting that the Legislature delegate" and urged the Legislature to "resolutely guard its constitutional role and authority." The LAO even wrote a letter to legislators identifying 12 separate attempts by Newsom to expand his own power and "sideline legislative authority." This well-regarded nonpartisan office later rebuked the Governor for "unilaterally appropriating" $200 million for homelessness, saying it set a "concerning precedent" when "the State Constitution entrusts the legislative branch with [this] power."

On May 21, I introduced Assembly Concurrent Resolution 196 to restore a balance of power between our branches. I pointed out that with a vaccine timeline of 12 to 18 months, allowing one-man rule to continue without limit would do grievous damage to our democratic institutions. I also argued that we could advance public health and economic recovery by making use of the Legislature's distinctive and complementary institutional strengths. The Los Angeles Times, in an editorial headlined "Time to cut off Gov. Newsom's blank check," stopped just short of endorsing the measure, saying "the governor needs to start sharing power again with the Legislature, as the state's constitution intends." Against the backdrop of this emerging consensus, James Gallagher (joint author of the Resolution) and I tried to begin a dialogue with the Governor.

Newsom would not engage at all, refusing to discuss any limits on his authority. Instead, he deputized his Legislative Affairs Secretary to accuse us of attempting "to prematurely declare an end to this ongoing crisis that has killed nearly 100,000 Americans, including more than 3,700 Californians." We were told condescendingly that Newsom hoped we too "will return [our] focus to this important work," even as he insisted all powers of the state were in his own hands.

The Third Branch

It's often said that in our legal system, the wheels of justice grind slowly. But in our case against the Governor we got an immediate result. On June 12, the day after filing the lawsuit, we obtained a Temporary Restraining Order enjoining the enforcement of Newsom's latest Executive Order, N-67-20. The Honorable Perry Parker, a State Superior Court Judge, also restrained the Governor from further usurpations of legislative authority.

I was not prepared for the sheer force of the public reaction. While we received criticism in some quarters, there was a widespread sense of elation, even from people who didn't know exactly what the case was about. For the first time in months, the voice of someone other than Gavin Newsom mattered. The reported death of the other two branches of government, to paraphrase Mark Twain, had perhaps been exaggerated. A semblance of our cherished American institutions had returned. It was like driving all night through a remote stretch of highway where the radio is all static, and then suddenly you're almost within range and can hear the faint rhythm of music.

This was Newsom's first loss in court, and the import of the ruling was clear: The era of one-man rule was over. Rather than accept the judgment, however, he rushed to the Court of Appeal. That prompted a sharp rebuke from the Orange County Register. Its editorial headlined "Court right to nix Gov. Newsom's executive order on voting" advised Newsom to "stop trying to defend the indefensible." It continued, "Instead of doubling down on executive orders that exceed his authority, he should focus on gaining approval for those legislative approaches." While the appeals court would eventually set aside the immediate relief on an obscure and curious technical basis, our case was soon thereafter set for a full-blown trial on the merits: the first real test of Newsom's emergency powers.

James Gallagher and I had been representing ourselves *in pro per*—that is, acting as our own attorneys. We are both lawyers by trade, although I hadn't practiced since joining the Legislature. (I've joked that my career trajectory just keeps getting worse: from teacher to lawyer to politician.) With a couple months until the trial, we decided we'd continue to handle the case on our own. At that point, there had only been a few filings; by now, several months later, James and I have together written hundreds of pages of briefs in addition to oral arguments, the trial, and all of the other mechanics of litigation. Sometimes, this has meant working at a frenetic pace, emailing the same document back and forth to each other dozens of times, adding material up until seconds before the filing deadline. If we were billing someone by the hour, we'd probably be millionaires several times over.

To be honest, this has been challenging on top of our other responsibilities. But it's vital to what we're trying to accomplish. This case is about standing up for our branch of government, and more importantly, for the people of California we were elected to serve, who have been denied the representative government that is every American's birthright. By representing ourselves in court, we are really representing our constituents in the only way we now can. As Newsom's legal team has strained to distort the law into an authoritarian mold, we've tried to infuse it with the voices of millions of Californians who have been disenfranchised and dispossessed. That's a task that could not be outsourced to an attorney-for-hire.

* * *

With the October 21 trial date approaching, the case was reassigned to a new judge. Governor Newsom had ousted the judge who ruled against him, filing a section 170.6 motion to "disqualify" Judge Parker on the ground that he was "prejudiced against defendant's interest in this action." As the only evidence for this extreme allegation, the Governor cited Parker's prior ruling. Apparently, having the nerve to restrain Gavin Newsom's power was itself enough for a Superior Court Judge who had served honorably for 30 years to suddenly become unfit to preside over the case. While the motion was a standard one available to litigants, it nevertheless felt like an attack on the independence of the judiciary, especially as Newsom argued (to the new judge) that the State of Emergency "centralizes the State's powers" in his hands.

This was the type of argument he had to make to defend orders that contradicted the plain terms of the Constitution and were obviously not urgent measures. As another example, Newsom asserted that "no evidence at all" was needed to justify his actions because the threat of the pandemic was "readily apparent." That premise, if accepted, would entirely sideline the courts as well as the Legislature for the duration of the State of Emergency. Citizens would lose any opportunity to vindicate their rights either through an elected representative or before a neutral adjudicator.

The Emergency Services Act does indeed give broad powers to a California Governor. It's a remarkable statute. But what's even more remarkable is that Newsom had still far exceeded what the Act allows. He was trying to turn it into a bottomless well of authority in a way no Governor had ever dreamed of. For instance, in some circumstances the Act allows a Governor to suspend a law's enforcement. But Newsom was using it to create entirely new laws, laying claim to unrestricted "police powers" and a "plenary authority to govern." This is the very definition of rule by fiat, a dictatorship in the Roman mold. It's something our system of government has never contemplated. Yet it's how Newsom, by his own account, conceived of his ubiquitous role in California life during the preceding months and into the indefinite future.

The polite way we framed this in our brief for the trial was that Newsom had "fallen into the habit of acting unilaterally" even for non-emergency purposes. We told the Superior Court he had used the State of Emergency to normalize one-man rule, issuing decrees "as a default mode of operation." Shortly after we wrote this, as if to prove the point, Newsom issued an Executive Order banning gas-powered vehicles by 2035. With wildfires out of control, the Governor wanted a positive headline, so he simply pronounced the ban. "California will be leading the nation in this effort," he declared, echoing the press release for his vote-by-mail order. Newsom imposed the ban unilaterally even though the Legislature had considered and declined to pass similar legislation earlier in the year—perhaps recognizing that the future of clean energy is advancing rapidly through the work of entrepreneurs an innovators, not vainglorious politicians—and even though it was a clear violation of federal law.

Newsom also used the catastrophic fires to try to get an upper hand in our case, claiming any limits on his emergency powers would "throw into chaos current efforts to combat the wildfires now burning across the State." It was a cynical, thinly veiled attempt to strike a chord with a Northern California court at a time of untold suffering in the region. And it had no merit at all: Governors had been fighting wildfires for years without transforming the state into an autocracy.

* * *

When I arrived at the Sutter County courthouse on October 21, the morning of the trial, I was met by a large crowd that had come from all around the state. There were only a few seats available in the courtroom so the court lotteried them off. Everyone else was able to watch a livestream, and the court, to its great credit, took the unusual step of streaming the trial on Facebook. By the Sacramento Bee's count, over 200,000 people tuned in.

This public interest reflected the amazing support James and I had gotten from countless Californians who sent their well-wishes and prayers. As we toiled with the unglamorous work of seemingly endless brief-writing and trial preparation, it was a tremendous source of inspiration. People from all walks of life and political persuasions were asking me about the case all the time. Many said they voted for Newsom but were horrified by what was happening to our state. It affirmed my belief that the case could be a unifying moment where we renewed our commitment to shared principles.

This idea, of bringing together our divided state, was so important to me that it's how I began my opening statement: "I believe that these foundational principles—separation of powers, the rule of law, republican government—ought to be unifying, ought to cut through the cacophony and the dissension and the vitriol that characterizes our politics now more than ever. It is my hope that having this public debate, resolving this issue in a public forum, can commit us anew to these principles and will have a salutary effect on the state of politics in society in the California of 2020."

But ultimately, the case was about the specific actions of Gavin Newsom. If the executive branch could openly assume the powers of another branch of government without correction by the third, then our Constitution would be reduced to parchment. I told the Court that "the laws of the State of California do not countenance an autocracy under any circumstances; they do not allow for one-person rule; they do not empower a Governor to legislate. Not for one day, and certainly not for eight months with no end in sight." I asked the Judge to reject a form of power that exalts the will of one man above all—"above our sacrosanct founding documents, above our carefully nurtured institutions, above the rule of law itself."

In his closing argument, Newsom's attorney remarked that these principles work well "in theory." I responded that over two centuries of American history show they work pretty well in practice too.

* * *

On November 2, 2020, Judge Sarah Heckman issued her ruling. She held that Governor Newsom had violated the State Constitution with Executive Order N-67-20. She noted that several other orders also violated the Constitution. Most importantly, she issued a permanent injunction restraining the Governor from further unconstitutional orders.

While Newsom argued that the Emergency Services Act transforms California into an autocracy and places all powers of the State in his hands, Judge Heckman held that its "plain meaning" does not "give the Governor the power to legislate." While Newsom argued against any restraints on his future conduct, Judge Heckman found it was "reasonably probable the Governor will continue issuing executive orders...violating the California Constitution." While Newsom had ousted Judge Parker for ruling he acted unlawfully, Judge Heckman reached the same conclusion. James and I released a joint statement, saying that "nobody disputes that there are actions that should be taken to keep people safe during an emergency. But that doesn't mean that we put our Constitution and free society on hold by centralizing all power in the hands of one man." Newsom's office offered a statement of its own: "We strongly disagree with specific limitations the ruling places on the exercise of the Governor's emergency authority."

Before our trial no California court had ever ruled a governor abused his emergency powers. The reason for that, of course, is that never before had we had a governor literally declare himself an autocrat. At the time of this writing, the case is on appeal, and the stakes are now higher than before. The decision will be binding on any Superior Court in any of California's 58 counties and will be the key precedent for direct challenges to any of Newsom's other emergency orders. As Phil Willon of the LA Times wrote, "I expect this case to wind up at the California Supreme Court. If so it would be one of the biggest checks on the California governor's executive authority in times of state emergencies."

* * *

Gavin Newsom is not the only governor to receive criticism for overstepping his powers in the COVID era. But he has clearly set himself apart through the brazenness of his actions and their avowedly political purpose. In late December, the Los Angeles Daily News published an editorial headlined "A needed challenge to Newsom's one-man rule." Calling our case a "high-stakes legal battle" testing "the limits of a governor's powers during an emergency, if there are any limits," the editorial described what is unique about Newsom's abuses: "Newsom has made statements that indicate his willingness to use the emergency to make permanent changes in California. He has suggested that COVID-19 is an 'opportunity to reshape the way we do business and how we govern' and spoken of using it to bring in a 'new progressive era.'"

"That suggests," the editorial concludes, "that the concentration of unlimited power in the hands of one individual is an emergency in itself."

CHAPTER SIX

Corrupt

"Almost every single major intractable problem, at the back of it you see a big money interest for whom stopping progress, stopping justice is really important to their bottom line." – *Tom Steyer*

Most Californians were first introduced to Tom Steyer by his plaid ties and offbeat debate performances in a vanity campaign for the 2020 Democrat presidential nomination. Although a genuine billionaire, he only had a net worth of a billion or two, making him an underdog even in the billionaires' bracket of a contest that included Mike Bloomberg. As it happened, neither tycoon did well, and Steyer, a former hedge fund manager, dropped out of the race in February. He managed to spend $250 million of his own money and get in a shouting match with Joe Biden in South Carolina while never presenting much of a rationale for being our next president.

If you are someone closely involved in politics, however, you were familiar with Tom Steyer long before this. He had been throwing huge sums of money around—exclusively to one side—for many years. Even before spending $75 million on a "Need to Impeach" campaign he launched within nine months of the President's inauguration, he was the single largest Democrat political donor of all time. As of July 8, 2019, he had contributed $247,950,992 to candidates, PACs, and other political groups. Most of it went to the kind of independent expenditures that the infamous *Citizens United* Supreme Court decision legalized, although he also wrote checks directly to dozens of California politicians.

After dropping out of the presidential race, Steyer kept a low profile in the early months of 2020. So it was quite a surprise to see him standing next to Gavin Newsom at the Governor's April 17 press conference. The reason for his presence was even more baffling: Newsom had tapped Steyer, described as a "civic leader," to chair a newly assembled 80-member "Task Force on Business and Jobs Recovery." The commission was charged with helping "Californians recover as fast as safely possible from the COVID-19 induced recession and to shape a fair, green, and prosperous future."

It appeared Newsom was treating one of the most important tasks ever to face any state—bringing the world's fifth largest economy back to life—as the mother of all patronage opportunities. As someone who had done everything I could to work towards a cohesive and bipartisan COVID response, I was mortified. "We needed a unifying nonpartisan figure to lead our economic recovery," I said in a statement. "By anointing the nation's biggest partisan political donor, it's hard to imagine Gov. Newsom more wildly missing the mark."

Given Steyer's funding of initiatives like the Green New Deal, his selection struck many as a move towards the "new progressive era" Newsom had promised he would use the coronavirus crisis to deliver. The "torrent of progressive words and phrases" from Newsom, Steyer, and other task force members at the press conference did not discourage that impression. One commentator suggested "the task force is not there to reopen the California economy as much as it is to remake it." Dan Walters observed that if the goal were truly economic recovery, "Steyer, with his penchant for ideological confrontation, in the driver's seat is probably more an impediment than a lubricant." In this respect, the selection solidified Newsom's standing as the nation's most partisan governor, to be discussed in Chapter 9. But above all what it highlighted, given Steyer's unrivaled mega-donor status, was Newsom's readiness to give access and influence to the highest bidder.

Steyer was actually an atypical example of this tendency. As much as billionaires are villainized for their political activities, they don't have enormous influence at the California Capitol, at least not in a systemic way. Wealthy individuals on the whole, in fact, are a relatively minor source of funding. The real influence lies not with individuals like the Steyer Commission's chair, but with entities like its members: major companies, industry associations, and most of all, massive union conglomerates. This latter Special Interest, which got 14 of the 80 spots on the commission, has the unique luxury of being able to conscript people into its ranks and take a cut of every paycheck. That's the mechanism by which these sprawling entities dominate our state's politics, outspending everyone else by a mile. One report showed the California Teachers Association spent twice as much electing California politicians as the next biggest spender—also a union conglomerate.

While Jerry Brown had a mixed relationship with "labor," as it is euphemistically called, with Gavin Newsom there was no ambiguity. This Special Interest was even more responsible than PG&E for his rise to power. In the 2018 campaign, the CTA spent millions supporting Newsom, and a large assortment of other labor associations wrote him checks for the $29,200 maximum. In his first year as Governor, Newsom returned the favor by going to war against charter schools and signing AB 5, among other rewards.

This dynamic was not disrupted by COVID-19. If anything, it was intensified by an escalation of the stakes. For the remainder of 2020, Newsom's solicitude for his biggest funders would drive pandemic-related policy in crucial ways. This, combined with the Governor's assumption of unprecedented power, would produce hardships in California without equal in the COVID era.

A Double Whammy

Governor Newsom issued his original stay-at-home order on March 19. Even before that, it was apparent that AB 5—the independent contracting ban written by the AFL-CIO and other union conglomerates—was compounding the public health and economic crises of COVID-19 to the point of absurdity. It was impossible for most people to work outside the home, yet the new law made it impossible for many people to work inside the home. If you were to try to invent a policy that was maximally incompatible with a statewide lockdown, AB 5 would be hard to beat.

Beyond that, there were soon reports that the law was "keeping needed health care personnel from working." On March 12, I wrote a letter to Governor Newsom asking that the law at least be suspended. "Recently enacted limitations on independent contracting—the likes of which exist in no other state—are causing a loss of flexibility over the time and place of work and a reduction in economic opportunity for as many as a million Californians," the letter said. In addition, AB 5 was making "the provision of care more difficult for physician assistants, nurse practitioners, respiratory therapists, radiology technicians, medical translators, home health providers, elder aides, and other professionals."

In a single day, I received hundreds more testimonials from Californians who said freedom from the scourge of AB 5 would allow them to cope with the emergency conditions, contribute to economy activity, and perform vital public health services. A woman named Kirstin said, "No online companies are hiring Californians right now. I'm losing my ten-year old business and can't make ends' meet. The health crisis + AB 5 is a double whammy. I won't survive in this state." An association representing tens of thousands of writers and photographers reported that "the financial devastation that our

California members have experienced in the wake of AB 5 has been compounded exponentially by the economic strife surrounding the COVID-19 crisis." I shared all of these testimonials with Governor Newsom, along with a letter from 200 Ph.D. economists urging him to suspend the law's enforcement.

It was all for naught. Newsom ignored these cries for help and insisted on keeping AB 5 in place. If that were the end of the story, it would be bad enough. But the Governor then exploited this moment of unique vulnerability for California workers to ruthlessly hammer the law in and advance its corrupt purposes.

While his EDD unemployment office has become the national poster child for government failure (as we will see in Chapter 8), the office's incompetence may have been exceeded by its malevolence. A website called *The People v. AB 5* (run by four self-described "Democrats who support unions" but were ardent opponents of the law) explained how the EDD "attempted to weaponize the COVID-19 crisis by leading out-of-work Californians into [a] trap." Instead of giving them access to benefits Congress included for independent contractors in the CARES Act, Newsom's EDD try to shoehorn them into the regular unemployment system where they would have to name names of their business partners. Once it had that list, EDD would pounce, launching audits of the named businesses for allegedly violating AB 5 and hitting them with fines ranging from $5,000 to $25,000 per "misclassification"—applied retroactively to before the law even existed. The site gave an example of a small "princess-for-your-little-girl's-birthday-party business" whose owner was audited and fined $60,000 dating back several years.

Incredibly, as small businesses were on their last legs, the EDD plowed ahead with these harassing audits using personnel that could have been processing unemployment claims. I wrote a letter to the Director and the Governor asking them to cut it out. The EDD Director,

Sharon Hilliard, wrote me back that the audits "must continue" even during the shutdown. The worst consequence of all of this was that countless freelancers—forced out of work by AB 5, COVID, or some combination of the two—had to wait weeks or months for benefits as the EDD played its political games to cater to Newsom's Special Interest backers. I heard from several people who couldn't put food on the table for their families.

But it got worse. On May 14, 2020, Newsom released his revised budget. The state was facing a $54 billion shortfall. Every dollar was precious. Yet in a budget that included basically nothing to support small businesses or job creation—and with California, throughout the COVID era, having about the worst unemployment in the country—the Governor found $21 million to specifically fund the enforcement of AB 5 so that more independent contractors would lose their livelihoods. He put three separate agencies on the job: the EDD, the Department of Industrial Relations, and the Department of Justice. It was the single most indecent act I had ever seen during my time in politics.

On the one occasion that the Assembly convened to consider the budget, I spoke directly to Newsom's $21 million AB 5 line-item. "Let's be very clear about what this is," I said. "This is $21 million to take aim at small businesses—to audit and prosecute them, to fine and penalize them, to harass and bully them—when they are struggling to survive like never before. It's $21 million to finish the job of decimating a community of independent professionals as diverse as California itself: spanning hundreds of professions—many of the most talented people in our state, many of the most vulnerable people in our state. It's $21 million to shut down gainful work and destroy livelihoods when we have more unemployed Californians than the total population of half the states in the country."

I then read to my colleagues the story of Monica from Chapter 2, the cancer survivor who sometimes felt like she wanted to die because of how AB 5 had ruined her life. "Governor Newsom doesn't care about Monica," I continued. "Governor Newsom has denied that people like Monica even exist. Governor Newsom is all too willing to create many more Monicas as a rich reward for the Special Interests with the most juice at this Capitol."

"Twenty-one million dollars—it's one line-item, one line-item in a sprawling budget. Yet there is so much dishonor packed into that one line, coiled more tightly than a strand of DNA, it tells you everything about what's become of California government."

It's Not About the Kids

The CTA has long been California's top political spender, and the UTLA, short for United Teachers of Los Angeles, is its largest affiliate. I used to be a UTLA member, when I taught 10th-grade English at a school in inner-city LA. Nowadays, thanks to the United States Supreme Court's decision in *Janus v. AFSCME*, I would have the right to opt out of the union, although California politicians have done everything in their power to make this difficult. The legal issue in *Janus*, incidentally, first came before the Supreme Court in a lawsuit against the CTA itself, but the Court deadlocked 4-4 after Justice Scalia's death.

On July 9, 2020, the UTLA published a 17-page "Research Paper" that was something between a manifesto and a hostage note. The debate over when to reopen schools was raging across the state, and the union set forth a list of demands before it would let that happen, including Medicare for All, defunding the police, overturning Proposition 13, imposing a wealth tax, and killing off charter schools. Borrowing Newsom's language, UTLA said the coronavirus was "an opportunity to create a new normal." The CTA as a whole had already demanded a new tax on billionaires as one prerequisite to reopening.

The game plan was clear. The unions would keep schools closed as long as possible and extract a heavy price for reopening. The first stage of this plan, getting the Governor in line, was easy enough. While he said on July 14 that a statewide order would not work because each district is "unique and distinctive," that statement proved no obstacle. Just three days later, Newsom did a complete 180, shutting down schools for over 90 percent of the state's students and overriding local decisions. To be fair, he did have one of his education advisors call me, as Vice Chair of the Education Committee, for "input" the day before the announcement—after the decision had clearly been made.

* * *

At this point, four months into COVID, Newsom had already more than gone to bat for the CTA. At the 11th hour of the budget process in June, he was party to a surprise "trailer bill" that eviscerated the one meaningful driver of school quality in California. A long-time equity advocate put it this way: "In my 30 years of close involvement in the state budget process, I've never witnessed such an egregious abuse." The bill stopped schools that enroll new students from receiving funding for them, which was unprecedented: funding has always followed the student in our public-school system. That's why it's called "per pupil." This was obviously harmful for growing communities, and it hurt school districts that attract families to the community by serving students well. But it was most devastating for charter schools—and that was the point.

Contrary to commonly peddled propaganda, charters are public schools. What's different about them is they aren't automatically assigned students in the surrounding neighborhood, as traditional schools are. They aren't assigned any students. They have to attract families to opt-in with a desirable product. And many were doing that more successfully than ever during COVID after pioneering distance learning models. Some charters had enrolled hundreds of new students for the coming school year. The Newsom-CTA trailer bill was designed to send those kids back to their neighborhood school, which in many underserved communities meant returning to the failing school they were trying to escape from. For good measure, the bill also barred non-classroom-based charters from billions in federal coronavirus relief.

To try to head off this attack on the very foundation of the charter school community, I gave perhaps my most impassioned speech ever on the Assembly Floor. "Again and again, time after time, we've had bills that target this community," I said. "This legislation only make sense in light of that invidious pattern of discrimination. The parents, and families, and school leaders, and teachers and everyone else who are part of this community, they look upon our state government with nothing but fear. They just wonder, what next? What harm is going to be done to me and my school and my way of life from the rarefied proceedings of this chamber. That's a dynamic that should never exist in a modern liberal democracy, yet this bill intensifies it like never before."

Unbothered, Newsom signed the bill. Soon thereafter he was sued in what was called "the most important civil rights education case since Brown v. Board of Education," the case that had overturned the doctrine of separate but equal. "I opened a network of schools to close the African American achievement gap by preparing kids for college in a different way," said Margaret Fortune, one of the plaintiffs. "We enter into this lawsuit, not lightly. But we will use every resource within our grasp to protect our children and our students."

Facing this lawsuit, Newsom was forced to backtrack on some of the bill's harmful provisions. But as my speech alluded to, it was just another front in the war on charters he had started his first year. In a move condemned by civil rights groups, he had signed a package of bills specifically designed to stop them from opening. The Urban Leagues of Greater Sacramento, San Diego, and Los Angeles described the bills as "a direct attack to the ability of African American parents to choose the best education possible for their children," adding: "It is not fair to African American families to take away public charter schools and force them back into failing district-run schools." Three chapters of the NAACP passed a resolution stating that "African American families are more likely to choose public charter schools" and that "African American students enrolled in public charter schools achieve academic outcomes exceeding their peers in district-run schools."

The reason Newsom has it out for charter schools is because unionization is voluntary, not automatic. The CTA and related associations have become behemoths by taking a cut of every public-school teacher's paycheck, and then funneling a large part of that revenue to Newsom and other politicians. Charters are a direct threat to that business model, no matter that they have proven to be the best hope for many underprivileged kids.

* * *

That the school shutdown fight would be drawn upon the same battle lines as the charter wars became clear just a few weeks into the COVID era. On March 26, UTLA wrote a letter to the district's superintendent to "demand a moratorium on the approval of any new charter schools." While "incoherently stoking coronavirus fears," Larry Sand of the Teachers Empowerment Network pointed out, the union was advancing the same demand for which it had orchestrated a district-wide strike the previous year. UTLA's letter nonsensically "labeled charter students, families, and staff as unique hazards to public health, stoking perverse and unfounded division," one equity advocate wrote.

Yet as the prospect of a long-term school shutdown came into focus,

CTA and its affiliates and enablers came to realize the stakes were even higher. This was their Super Bowl. In early July, with Step 1 complete (instruct Newsom to close schools), the CTA moved to Step 2, "calling on lawmakers to adopt additional revenues," including "suspension of corporate tax credits, capturing unrealized capital gains or imposing a tax on the wealthiest billionaires and millionaires." The CTA and other union conglomerates are always the main proponents for tax increases, because that puts more money on the table to negotiate for—and through their campaign activities, they've selected who sits on the "other side" of the table.

At the same time, the CTA saw to it that even the tiny fraction of districts that could, in theory, proceed with some form of reopening under the Governor's order would not do so, lest it start a trend. The union parachuted in to even the smallest districts. I spoke with one district official, whose district was so small CTA had never bothered much with it, that was suddenly dealing with a top state-level negotiator. Local school board members were being vilified for trying to offer any classroom-based option.

Yet the desire of parents, students, and teachers was clear: I surveyed my district, and of the 6,028 people who responded, 80 percent wanted an in-person learning option to start the school year. To try to deflate this public pressure, the CTA drew an absolute line and deemed any deviation from a total shutdown to be intolerable. After LA public health authorities cleared students with special needs and English language learners to return to school, UTLA still tried to stop it. Meanwhile, private elementary schools were reopening in large numbers, as they were able to serve local families without interference by Sacramento Special Interests.

But pressure to open schools kept growing. On October 14, the mayors of California's 13 largest cities urged the state to act "quickly and intentionally" to open schools. In San Francisco, where the district was spending its time on a "blue ribbon commission" to take the names of insufficiently woke figures like Abraham Lincoln and Dianne Feinstein off of schools sites, Mayor London Breed issued a blistering statement saying the district needed to "focus on reopening our public schools, not renaming them."

Faced with this emerging consensus—along with the pellucidly clear science, to be discussed in the next chapter—Newsom, the CTA, and their allies dug in, inventing new reasons keep schools closed. A trio of Sacramento unions previewed the new strategy in a letter declaring that even schools that could safely open must remain closed until at least 2021 so that no one gets "a head start." At an October 14 hearing, I asked the State Superintendent of Public Instruction Tony Thurmond, a close Newsom ally whom the CTA had groomed for the post, to disavow keeping schools closed for reasons unrelated to COVID. He would not. To the contrary, Thurmond tipped his hand that the plan was to keep many schools closed the entire academic year or longer, breathlessly citing "new data" that "COVID could be with us well beyond 2021."

As 2020 drew to a close, the CTA launched a statewide disinformation campaign to keep schools closed. Teachers throughout the state were blasted with text messages urging them to "call Governor Newsom" and "tell him that no school in counties with COVID-19 rates in the Purple tier should be open for in-person instruction." The text ticked off a laundry list of preconditions for reopening: "accountability, transparency, and enforceability of all state safety guidelines," the ability to "monitor, investigate, and enforce all safety standards," and "accurate and transparent data on COVID transmission rates in schools." The union's leadership also put out a cryptic letter declaring that "[s]afety and transparency should not be the minimum standard. They should be our maximum goals." Ominously, the letter continued, "Safety is not just a today issue. Safety protocols will need to be in place while we wait for, through and even after widespread distribution of the COVID-19 vaccine."

Newsom got the message. On December 30, 2020 he called a special press conference to roll out a new "Safe Schools for All" plan. In fact, the plan did not open schools for anyone, instead simply promising $2 billion in eventual funding for elementary schools. It also added new barriers and costs for school districts, proposed new penalties that would quickly become a weapon in the hands of school closure interests, and failed to mention middle and high schools at all. It was a classic Gavin Newsom announcement: aimed at getting a big headline while doing next to nothing and keeping Special Interests happy.

* * *

Letting our state's top campaign contributor dictate school closures was the very definition of politics over science. And for me, it was personal. I taught high school in inner-city LA and ran for the Legislature to fight for quality public schools. But as Vice Chair of the Assembly Education Committee, every attempt I'd made to expand opportunity had been thwarted by the CTA and its enablers at the Capitol. The school closure debate put in sharp relief the central reality of California's soulless education politics. It's not—it's never—about the kids.

The Room Where It Happens

The source of power for the CTA, other union conglomerates, and the broader constellation of Sacramento Special Interests is political contributions. But their instrument for translating these contributions into tangible policy outcomes is a corps of lobbyists whose offices encircle the Capitol—known collectively as the "Third House" because of the control they exert over the first two houses, the Assembly and the Senate. Every legislator gets hundreds of thousands of dollars from the Third House, doled out at regular "events" that Legislators hold at restaurants around the Capitol, usually costing at least $2,000 per ticket with alcohol flowing freely.

Gavin Newsom's infamous dinner at the French Laundry restaurant put this aspect of Sacramento's political culture on shocking display. As the Sacramento Bee Editorial Board wrote, "Newsom paid hundreds of dollars—and knowingly risked political scandal—to attend a feast with lobbyists. The French Laundry photos provided a glimpse of the behind-the-scenes world in which powerful interests can privately cajole California's chief executive over wine and nosh." In a story headlined "Newsom's French Laundry dinner shows how lobbyists get access to power in Sacramento," the San Francisco Chronicle noted that the dinner "highlighted the close ties and revolving door of government that make Sacramento turn, frustrating those who can't be in the room where it happens." Jessica Levinson, former president of the Los Angeles Ethics Commission, described the event as "the equivalent of a big sign to the public that says, 'You're not welcome at this table.'"

The "French Laundry crew," as the Bee described those around the table, was a cast of Third House notables. Photos from the dinner showed Newsom "in deep conversation with top lobbyists from the California Medical Association." The lobbyist whose birthday was being celebrated, Jason Kinney, was considered "a poster boy for the type of shadow influence that pervades Sacramento." He had earned $220,000 from PG&E's creditors to lobby Newsom on the creation of a $21 billion fund to help the utility emerge from bankruptcy. Emily Rusch of the California Public Interest Research Group said "it certainly can cause the public to question whether any advice the governor is getting is in the public interest or in the interest of the companies that have paid Kinney's firm to lobby."

Meanwhile, even beyond the enforcement of AB 5 and the closure of schools, the fingerprints of lobbyists seemed to be all over Newsom's COVID response. Kinney, the French Laundry honoree, succeeded in securing an exemption from Newsom's lockdowns for his Hollywood clients. In connection with the BYD affair, the prominent Sacramento lobbyist who represented the checkered company also represented "Bloom Energy, which the state [was] paying $2 million to refurbish ventilators; Blue Shield, the health care behemoth that dominates the task force Newsom assembled to increase testing for COVID-19; and NextGen America, the progressive advocacy group headed by Tom Steyer." In November, Newsom appointed a new Chief of Staff, Jim DeBoo, who was plucked from the upper echelons of the Third House. Jamie Court of Consumer Watchdog blasted the Governor for turning "over the keys to the castle to this big bucks lobbyist." The San Francisco Chronicle reported that many of Newsom's other staff members were also former lobbyists, including his legislative affairs secretary, his chief deputy legislative affairs secretary, and his chief deputy appointments secretary.

The French Laundry dinner presented such a disturbing image of Newsom as a stooge for lobbyists that he was forced to appoint a "Chief Ethics Advisor" to monitor his relationship with them. For the state's most powerful special interests and their well-heeled "advocates," the era of one-man rule was working out quite well.

* * *

When Tom Steyer announced he was running for President in August of 2019, he said that with "[a]lmost every single major intractable problem, at the back of it you see a big money interest for whom stopping progress, stopping justice is really important to their bottom line." Steyer was talking about Washington, D.C., but it was in his own backyard, at California's Capitol, where this corruption of our political life had reached a level beyond comparison—and where it was embodied by a Governor under whom Steyer would soon serve.

Steyer's commission, as it turned out, was as much of a bust as his presidential campaign. At the April press conference announcing its formation, Newsom had set high expectations. "We want to make this meaningful," he said. "This is not something where, in six months, I'm looking forward to giving you a draft or putting out a long, thick report." It was actually seven months, and what he gave us was a fairly thin report. On November 20, 2020, the commission was disbanded, quietly issuing a 27-page document titled "Recovery for All" with a series of anodyne recommendations.

This one and only report, Politico noted, contained "no specific new initiatives to protect California businesses in the pandemic," and it "was not immediately clear why Newsom was shutting down his task force just as California enters a new round of business closures." Over its "short life," the article continued, the "task force faced criticism from some business leaders who said that it appeared to be rudderless and provided little substance in terms of detailed planning." In August, the Los Angeles Times had reported that "months after the governor called together the task force...few details about its work have been made public," noting that the "task force has operated almost entirely behind closed doors" with Consumer Watchdog likening it to a "star chamber." Steve Maviglio, a Democratic strategist who was the press secretary for Gray Davis, remarked that the "idea was to bring California's best minds and brainpower. What's there to account for that?" The most memorable thing about the commission turned out to be Bob Iger of Disney's resignation from it in October.

The Steyer episode, while of little ultimate consequence, starkly illustrates the leadership failures of Gavin Newsom that have caused so much to go haywire with COVID in California: a tendency for splashy announcements that lead nowhere, a subservience to moneyed interests, a willingness to use crisis for political purposes, an excessive partisan zeal, a denial of public access, and, as we will now see, an ignorance of data and science on questions of monumental importance to 40 million Californians.

CHAPTER SEVEN

Unscientific

"Not that I had a particularly high opinion of it before, but the irrational and not-very-science-driven regime of COVID policies in California, coupled with the hypocrisy of so many elected officials there, has really lowered my opinion of the quality of governance in that state." – Nate Silver, 538

"When it comes to re-opening, SCIENCE – not politics – must be California's guide," Governor Gavin Newsom tweeted on April 14, 2020. Two weeks later, in an apparent shot at Andrew Cuomo, Newsom tweeted, "The West Coast is – and will continue to be – guided by SCIENCE." On May 4 came: "CA is led by data and SCIENCE." On June 24: "This isn't about politics. It's about SCIENCE." The next day Newsom added, "Dr. Fauci is right – this isn't about politics. It's about SCIENCE." The tweet was not clear as to whether Dr. Fauci had himself screamed the word.

These were just the times the Governor gave science the all-caps treatment. Twenty-six other tweets made similar pronouncements at a conversational volume. While a purported adherence to science is not usually the stuff of social media chest-beating, the layers of irony ran deeper than that. With every edict from Sacramento—every new order, regulation, or guidance document; every reinvented taxonomy of tiers, phases, or colors; every addition or deletion of criteria, metrics, or indicators; every introduction of novel vocabulary, like attestation or emergency brake—California's COVID experience grew more surreal. Absent in all of this was the key feature of the scientific method: an "unwillingness to take unverified and untheorized claims about the world as truth, simply because someone states that they are true."

In Gavin Newsom's California, science was reduced to an incantation, an elixir, a shibboleth. It became a device for easy virtue signaling, a muzzle for silencing debate, a weapon for beating opponents over the head. It was a code serving to keep government secret and centralize authority; an all-purpose justifier for any policy no matter how political or self-serving; a trump card against any other human good, legal nicety, or even non-preferred scientific theory. It was made into a dog whistle for the unassailable orthodoxy—wall-to-wall lockdowns—rather than an invitation to inquiry and discovery. It stood as a barricade denying access, input, and democratic self-determination to the untutored masses who couldn't possibly have anything to contribute.

What resulted was not only a COVID-19 response with the nation's worst outcomes, but a diminishment of each enterprise, science and politics, along with their capacity for collaboration in a world fraught with uncertainty and peril.

A Day Not at the Beach

At the 28 minute and 29 second mark of his April 30 press conference, Governor Newsom told Orange County to pound sand. "We're going to do a hard close in that part of the state," Newsom said as he shut down the county's beaches. "They've done a wonderful job down there. I just think we can tighten that up a little bit."

Apparently forgetting the dictum that "the plural of anecdote is not data," Newsom cited a few "disturbing" images of OC beachgoers he had seen. He added that anyone who did not find the images concerning was not "paying attention to this pandemic and how it is spread." Asked for evidence of a "health impact of those crowds on the beaches," Newsom could not cite any. Nate Silver of 538 said that given "what we seem to be learning about outdoor transmission" Newsom's order would produce a public backlash "while not necessarily getting a huge amount of mileage in terms of public health." Local officials were "livid," with Michelle Steel, chairwoman of the Orange County Board of Supervisors, saying the order was based on a "few misleading pictures" and lacked any "rational basis." The Mayor of Newport Beach agreed the closure was not "grounded in data" as there was no showing that beaches were a "direct threat to health and safety." He added that Newsom did not speak "to a single local official" and "substituted his will for our judgment from 428 miles away in Sacramento."

The Associated Press described the beach closure announcement as a "clumsy rollout." The night before, word had gotten out via a memo from the California Highway Patrol that all beaches in the whole state would be closed. After receiving pushback from other coastal lawmakers, Newsom decided to single out Orange County. Yet at the press conference, he flatly denied he had considered the statewide order at all. This was a lie, as Politico reported in a story headlined "Newsom considered statewide beach closure despite publicly dismissing idea." Other states, meanwhile, were not closing beaches at all. Thus began a pattern: Newsom failing to justify a uniquely restrictive action while misleading the public and ignoring data-based input from local communities even as he claimed the mantle of scientific veracity—yielding disastrous consequences for public health.

* * *

California "has had the strictest regulations throughout the lockdown." The state is an outlier not only in the overall extent and duration of restrictions, but also with respect to a number of specific activities. For instance, California has been one of only a few states not to allow bowling, with its inherent social distancing. We were one of three states to forbid youth sports. We had one of the only state-imposed curfews and one of the only statewide school closure orders. Newsom had little company in banning outdoor dining and closing playgrounds, though he quickly reversed himself on the latter after some lawmakers protested.

The head of the state restaurant association reported that California's "most restrictive" lockdown was "inflicting the most devastation" anywhere in the country "on small businesses and the most economically vulnerable service workers." The state's economy was in extended freefall as a result, with nearly the worst unemployment rate in the country throughout the pandemic. In the last week of August, for instance, California accounted for 25 percent of the nation's unemployment claims while having only 12 percent of its population. As one of countless examples, Garth Gilmour, owner of a home wireless and security small business, said he had to "lay off all of my employees after having exhausted PPP and SBA loans but at least I will have tried to achieve the no-longer-achievable American dream." Yet perversely, by December California was also the leading COVID-19 hotspot, with by far the worst case rate in the country. In fact, cases would have been declining nationwide if not for California overwhelming that trend. "By any calculation, California's outbreak numbers are stunning," Politico reported.

But there had been no reason to expect Newsom's approach would work, since he refused to provide evidence for it. Nate Silver, considered by many the high priest of data science, criticized the "irrational and not-very-science-driven regime of COVID policies in California," adding, as a New Yorker, "Don't mistake us for California." The California Business Roundtable repeatedly asked Newsom for data "that would show how business openings have affected COVID rates and transmission." He would not provide it. A judge in Los Angeles County struck down an outdoor dining ban as "not grounded in science, evidence, or logic," yet Newsom thought it was such a good idea he applied it statewide. A San Diego Court then came to the same conclusion: "Given every opportunity, the State has provided the Court with no evidence" to justify outdoor dining restrictions. Underscoring this arbitrariness, a video posted by a sobbing Los Angeles restaurant owner showed that the filmset for NBC Universal's "Good Girls," complete with outdoor dining, was operating free and clear within feet of her shuttered location. "Everything I own is being taken away from me and they set up a movie company right next to my outdoor patio," she said. Her video received 9.6 million views on Twitter.

It became increasingly clear that Newsom's restrictions were not just inflicting needless harm but backfiring and contributing to spread of the virus. From the earliest days, he offered guidance that turned out to be off base. In a March 30 Daily Show appearance, he confidently implored millions of viewers to start "making better decisions" by avoiding four specific activities, all of an outdoors variety: "not going to the beach, or playgrounds, or parks" and "not going on a jog" when there were people around. As the distinction between indoor and outdoor transmission risks became even clearer, the state failed to take heed. Julia Marcus, an infectious-disease researcher at Harvard University, said while moving activities outdoors is crucial, many policies in California "actually do the opposite." Brown University health economist Emily Oster observed that "[s]ome of the things they're telling you not to do are incredibly low-risk. When you are so strict about what people can do, they stop listening."

"It's not because the public is irresponsible; it's because they are losing trust in public health officials who put out arbitrary restrictions," said Dr. Monica Gandhi, an infectious-disease specialist at UC San

Francisco. "California is unique because this particular lockdown came off as arbitrary and not data driven. Californians have listened to the news. They have seen the data on the virus, they know that being outside is safer, they know the impact the lockdown will have on businesses that could die forever, and they just don't buy it." Dr. Gandhi noted that opposition to the lockdown came from "medical professionals, lawmakers, parents and those with nuanced thinking who believe it's too restrictive, and didn't incorporate the biology of the virus."

In another counterproductive policy, Newsom deputized his Health and Human Services Secretary to announce a curfew. Yet the "virus doesn't care—day or night," said Mark Cullen, an infectious disease expert and former professor at Stanford University, calling the restriction "an odd one that doesn't in and of itself address the problem." Another infectious disease professor, Lee Riley, pointed out that curfews could drive more people indoors, especially younger people. Ellie Murray, an epidemiologist at Boston University's School of Public Health, said, "I've spoken with a lot of other epidemiologists and public health specialists, and we're not really sure at all where the justification in terms of the science for these curfews is." She added the effect of the curfew could just be to cram more people into a shorter time window.

To make matters worse, the rules kept changing in major ways without any coherent justification. On April 14, Newsom announced six "indicators" for modifying the stay-at-home order—testing, protection of high-risk populations, hospital surge capacity, therapeutic development, ability to support physical distancing, and ability to determine when to re-impose restrictions—which became the basis for a "Resilience Roadmap" consisting of four reopening "stages." On May 18, counties were given a "new attestation opportunity" where they could move to a new stage more quickly. Several did so, with local governments, businesses, and citizens putting a great deal of effort into adapting community life to the requirements for attestation. But on June 28, amid an uptick in cases, the Governor started closing whole categories of establishments statewide. Then, on August 28, came a lightning bolt from Mount Olympus: the Resilience Roadmap was out, supplanted by a totally new "Blueprint for a Safe Economy." The six "indicators" were replaced by two entirely different metrics: case rates and positivity rate, which would be used to assign counties to one of four color-coded "tiers." Counties were shuffled across these tiers for a few months until, on November 16, a new "emergency brake" was applied moving most of the state to the most restrictive "purple" tier. On November 21 came the curfew and then on December 3 a state-at-home order linked to yet another new metric: ICU capacity.

The whole point of setting criteria is to have a stable yardstick for evaluating variable data. I urged Governor Newsom to be transparent and work with the Legislature and local communities to get everyone on the same page and get things right. But instead, he resorted to unilateral, insular, haphazard decision-making, with the criteria in constant flux. The result was chaos, distrust, and needless suffering. The people of California, who had heroically risen to the occasion in March and April, were treated like clay in his hands, subject to zig-zagging, life-altering edicts lacking any basis in science. "It feels like during this whole pandemic, the people in charge have been acting like this is an experiment in a lab at Stanford," one advocate said.

But at least Newsom learned one thing. On December 10, 2020, with California going through the nation's worst COVID surge, he released some suggestions for safe activities. First on the list: "Go to a beach."

Killing Our Kids

One reason Newsom's COVID response was so unscientific is

that science was getting in the way of other political priorities. In the last chapter, we saw how a preternatural subservience to powerful Special Interests was the cause of his school closure policy. As much of an indictment as that is, even more damning is the effect: a tragedy for millions of California kids that mountains of scientific evidence warned against.

California schools were ordered closed statewide on April 1 and remained so through the summer. By the time the question of reopening for the new school year presented itself, the evidence was clear on three counts: the minimal risks to children from COVID-19, the enormous harms of extended school closures, and the negligible impact of school openings on community transmission. The day of Newsom's July school closure order, I released a statement citing evidence that "school closures do little to flatten the epidemic curve, while they are a calamity for kids." That evidence only became more rock solid in the latter half of 2020. Yet by the end of the year, Headmaster Newsom had still expelled the vast majority of students from the classroom.

* * *

A deadly virus is not always less deadly for kids. One of the few things to be grateful for in 2020 was that this particular virus turned out to be not very dangerous for them at all. The Journal of the American Medical Association reported in May that "the overall burden of COVID-19 infection in children remains relatively low" and that "children are at far greater risk of critical illness from influenza than from COVID-19."

By the time of Newsom's July 17 closure order, these limited risks from the virus were well-understood. Equally well-established were the wide-ranging and inequitably felt harms of keeping kids home from school. On June 29, the American Academy of Pediatrics "strongly advocate[d] that all policy considerations for the coming school year should start with a goal of having students physically present in school." In a 125-page report released on July 15, the National Academies of Sciences, Engineering, and Medicine concluded after weighing risks that "school districts should prioritize reopening schools full time." On July 24, the CDC joined the chorus with a statement on "the importance of reopening America's schools this fall." Even the New York Times published an editorial calling for schools to open, leaving Newsom torn between his two main constituencies: California special interests and the national news media.

As we saw in Chapter 6, Newsom stuck with the former. The most direct consequence has been substantial learning loss, with students losing between 50 and 100 percent of a whole year's worth of math in the Spring, according to the Brookings Institute. This was not experienced equally by all students: McKinsey found that "learning loss will exacerbate existing achievement gaps by 15 to 20 percent." Many kids in low-income areas never logged in for remote learning and were completely unaccounted for. Richard Rothstein, author of *The Color of Law: A Forgotten History of How Our Government Segregated*, wrote that closing schools would "take existing academic achievement differences between middle-class and low-income students and explode them," as kids with attentive parents would outpace those with a challenging home life. Dan Walters called it "nothing short of educational apartheid."

Yet the harms did not end there. The American Academy of Pediatrics cited other risks from school closures, including "child and adolescent physical or sexual abuse, substance use, depression, and suicidal ideation," placing kids "at considerable risk of morbidity and, in some cases, mortality." The depression and suicide fears have been tragically borne out, with mental-health related Emergency Room visits for minors increasing between 24 and 31 percent. I've personally heard from counties where utilization of youth mental health services went up 60 percent—a humanitarian crisis of the government's creation.

Most jarring, a November study by the Journal of the American Medical Association found that because learning loss diminishes life success, elementary school students across America had already lost 5.5 million years of life expectancy. It takes a fairly simple calculation to show what that finding would mean for California: Newsom's school closures have caused even greater loss of life than COVID-19. That's why Dan Walters wrote that school closures are "killing our kids."

* * *

Still, Newsom argued, keeping schools closed was necessary to stop the spread of COVID-19. It should first be recognized that even if this were true, we would be sacrificing our kids' education, development, health, and years of life to some other social objective—a morally uncomfortable proposition, to say the least.

But it's not true. Newsom's own Health and Human Services Secretary acknowledged this on October 6: "We have not seen a connection between increased transmission and school reopening," he said. That was certainly the experience of schools in the district I represent, and it's what the evidence had shown for months. As early as March, an Imperial College research team found school closures "hardly impact the epidemic curve." In April, another study found that "school closures alone had little effect on the speed and burden of the epidemic." A report out Finland and Sweden found "closure or not of schools had no measurable direct impact on the number of laboratory confirmed cases in school-aged children."

Fearmongering claims were repeatedly shot down. A study in the New England Journal of Medicine reported, "We have not found a single instance of a child infecting parents." Mark Woolhouse, an epidemiologist at the University of Edinburgh, said it is extremely difficult to find any instance anywhere in the world of a child transmitting to a teacher in school." On the strength of this evidence, Dr. Anthony Fauci recommended keeping schools open even as the country experienced a surge in the fall.

Governors across the country followed the evidence. On August 7, Andrew Cuomo cleared all 749 New York school districts to open. On October 27, the Secretary of Education in Massachusetts observed "it is increasingly clear that schools are not a source of transmission" and told even high-risk communities to keep schools open. Meanwhile, kids withered at home in California, in what Nate Silver, in a dramatic understatement, called a "not particularly science-driven" policy.

The Equity Metric

As Newsom widened inequities in our schools and throughout our state, on September 30 he made a startling announcement. Suddenly, he cared so much about "equity" that it became the name of an additional third metric for the Blueprint for a Safe Economy, which counties would have to satisfy before they could move up a tier. This new Equity Metric was possibly the most unscientific policy adopted anywhere in the COVID era.

No other state had anything resembling it. But that's not because other states don't care about equity. Based on their policies, they seem to care about it much more than California. We have the highest poverty rate in the country and the second worst income inequality (as measured by Gini coefficient), largely as a result of laws like AB 5 and other Special Interest payouts that limit opportunity and raise costs for ordinary California. Likewise, we have among the nation's worst educational achievement gaps because keeping kids trapped in failing schools supports the business model of our state's biggest political spender. As discussed in the previous two sections, these inequities have been radically amplified by Newsom's corrupt and unscientific COVID shutdown policies.

So on September 30, we had the setup for a typical Gavin Newsom announcement: seeking to grab a headline by making California the "first" to do something while sabotaging the purported goals of the initiative by letting Special Interests drive the policies that matter. But this day marked a new level of absurdity. Newsom was going to keep counties locked down if areas with marginally higher infection rates had lower voter turnout, fewer tree canopies, or less alcohol flowing than the rest of the county. Characteristics like these, among 25 "socioeconomic" factors in a so-called Healthy Places Index, would be used to score a county's dozens of census tracts. The lowest scoring fourth of these tracts would get cherry-picked from across the county and lumped together into one group. Then, the average COVID case rates for this purely invented subgroup could keep the county in a lower tier, even if the countywide averages merited advancement.

Under this scheme, two counties with identical case positivity rates could be subject to different restrictions based not on how cases were distributed physically—a plausible public health consideration—but on how that distribution lined up with voter turnout, environmental quality, proximity to bars, and other supposed socioeconomic factors. The freedom of whole counties would depend on minor differences between fabricated subdivisions in a grab bag of dubious characteristics.

Even if this scheme were measuring equity in some real sense, it would not have been the right way to combat some of the disproportionate impacts of COVID-19. The way to do that was what dozens of other states (as well as California to some extent) were already doing: targeting investments where they were needed to increase access to PPE or needed services. But Newsom took this idea in a chilling direction. Restricting the basic liberties of citizens to impose a notion of "equity" defined by the government is a move with some very bad precedents in world history.

Writing for CATO, Walter Olsen suspected the point of the new metric was to obtain "leverage with which to push counties into 'equity' initiatives that go beyond criteria of sound disease control." Such initiatives would surely wind up being the not-so-equitable kind that usually prevail at our Capitol. The long and short of it was that the most authoritarian "emergency power" claimed by Gavin Newsom—to shut down communities, shutter businesses, close schools, separate friends and family, and imprison citizens in their homes—was being used in service of political goals with no relation to public health.

* * *

When Gavin Newsom threw out the Resilience Roadmap in favor of the Blueprint, what angered many people most was that one color was missing. "We don't believe there's a green light that says go back to the way things were," the Governor said. Nothing could have been further from the truth. Coronavirus was a temporary problem; it was not the end of history. The Governor's fatalism was the height of hubris. Our collective future is never up to a single person, and certainly not a person who'd been so wrong at such a high cost to so many.

As it happened, Newsom was also taking steps to get in the way of the one thing scientists were saying was a green light: the vaccine. At an October 19 press conference, Newsom announced he was setting up a separate approval process that any FDA-approved COVID vaccine would have to pass before anyone could get it in California. "We're not going to take anyone's word for it," Newsom said, though we'd keep taking the FDA's word for every other drug. U.S. Senator Lamar Alexander, Chair of the Senate Health Committee, admonished Newsom to "stop second guessing" the "career scientists" at the FDA, which Alexander said would "delay approval, discourage Americans from taking the vaccine, and cost lives."

Newsom's disregard for science had made the COVID era as insufferable in California as anywhere. Now, his disrespect for scientists was going to keep the era from drawing to a merciful close.

CHAPTER EIGHT

Incompetent

"California has certainly not escaped this national crisis unscathed."
– Gavin Newsom, Dec. 30, 2020

On August 3, 2020, California Governor Gavin Newsom disappeared.

A figure who had been omnipresent in the lives of his people since March was not to be seen for an entire week. While there were shades of South Carolina Governor Mark Sanford's mysterious disappearance in 2009, the explanation turned out to be less salacious than a rendezvous with an Argentinian mistress. Newsom was simply hiding. Following a disastrous COVID "data glitch," he was apparently ensconced in his Fair Oaks estate as his Health and Human Services Secretary publicly apologized and his Public Health Director resigned.

Unfortunately for Newsom, the sudden disappearance card is one you can really only play once. He might have saved it for November 23. That's when county prosecutors—not state officials—uncovered "the most significant fraud of taxpayer funds in California history." It was something out of the Onion: while law-abiding Californians were waiting months for urgently needed unemployment benefits, checks were flying out the door to murderers and child molesters using names like Dianne Feinstein, Scott Peterson, and Poopy Britches to perpetrate their fraud.

These two events, both chapters in larger horror stories, encapsulated the COVID-19 experience for many Californians. Our

Governor was doing a great many things they could have done without, while neglecting the core functions that were now a matter of survival. He was draining the life out of our communities and then withholding life support, unraveling the structure of society and failing to pick up the pieces. Between talk show appearances and powwows with lobbyists, Newsom couldn't be bothered to get the state bureaucracy to competently serve the public. If anything, he interfered with its performance by politicizing agency operations.

What resulted was frustration, deprivation, despair—certainly a loss of faith in government—on a scale that even a contagious virus should not be able to inflict upon a modern democratic society, especially one with the technology, wealth, and human capital that ours had at its disposal. Rarely in history has a ball been so momentously dropped.

The EDD Train Wreck

"We're doing everything to try get those unemployment insurance checks out as quickly as possible," Gavin Newsom told Ellen DeGeneres during an April 17, 2020 appearance on her show.

In the months that followed, it was not clear what, if anything, the Governor had done. And on August 5, a bipartisan group of 61 California Legislators called him on it. In a scathing letter, the five dozen lawmakers—mostly of his own party—took Newsom to task for this "failure of our state government." They said they had "seen little progress over the last four months."

"In our fifth month of the pandemic, with so many constituents yet to receive a single unemployment payment, it's clear that EDD is failing California. Millions of our constituents have had no income for months," the letter read. "As Californians wait for answers from EDD, they have depleted their life savings, have gone into extreme debt, and are in deep panic as they figure out how to put food on the table and a roof over their heads." The lawmakers had "been met with long-winded excuses, fumbling non-answers, or unclear and inconsistent data," along with a "[l]ack of transparency and accountability," even "obfuscation and dishonesty" in their dealings with the agency. "We have exhausted all avenues at our disposal," they said.

For months many legislators had lashed out at the EDD while tiptoeing around putting blame directly on the Governor. This letter dispensed with any such pretense, pointing out the absurdity of Newsom's recent announcement where he committed to "focus on immediately processing claims." The lawmakers bluntly noted that this "begg[ed] the question of what EDD was doing before your announcement—if not 'focusing on immediately processing claims.'" They further accused the Governor of only addressing "a few of the many issues we have highlighted for months" and "only scratch[ing] the surface of the disaster that is EDD." The frustrated legislators said that given "how little has improved at EDD over the course of the pandemic," they were writing Newsom "out of a spirit of partnership, asking you take further action."

Newsom agreed to put together a "strike team." At 8:52 PM on September 19, a Saturday, the team produced an overdue report that—beyond the sky-is-blue conclusion that the EDD needed a complete overhaul—contained stunning revelations about pending claims. While the agency had said in July that its claims backlog would be cleared by September, the report found 1.5 million claims remained unresolved and the backlog was *increasing* by 10,000 each week. Now, new claims would not even be accepted for two weeks so EDD would be able to catch up by January.

It did not catch up. At the time of this writing in early January, the claims backlog was growing again and EDD had just suddenly suspended 1.4 million accounts. Newsom had presided over this train wreck for 10 months without improvement.

* * *

In late April, my office received a call from a woman named Emily who was inconsolable, saying she was on the brink of giving up hope. She was out of work and her EDD claim had been pending for a month. She had no money, no way to pay her bills or put food on the table. "I just can't do this anymore," she said, adding she couldn't "hang on the Governor's promises anymore." We would later learn the agency had made a basic processing error, denying her claim and not even telling her.

I could provide hundreds of other stories just like this. At times during 2020, my office would open dozens of new cases every day from constituents who couldn't get their benefits. Doing justice to their stories would take a book in itself. We heard from constituents who would call EDD hundreds of times with no answer; who received notices with someone else's social security number, employer, or earnings; who would wait weeks, months, or forever for their benefits. By one estimate, only one in a thousand people would reach a live person when they tried to call EDD. Sometimes, after finally getting through, the caller would be abruptly hung up on. The callback option routinely failed, with people requesting a callback and not getting one. No reason was given for benefit denials, and when one was given it often didn't make sense. One claimant had an *electronic* application denied as "illegible." Every legislative office was having the same experience; San Francisco Assemblyman David Chiu, a Democrat, started a #EDDFailoftheDay hashtag featuring the worst incidents.

Part of the problem was EDD's obsolete technology. There were system crashes, delays, and innumerable glitches in what the LA Times called "a perfect storm of failures for a state government with a long history of technology problems." For years, the nonpartisan Legislative Analyst's Office had reported on EDD's "aging and inflexible" IT system. As of 2020, the agency was four years into an 11-year, $30 million "modernization" of its software and was still in the planning stages. Other states had made immediate improvements by partnering with the private sector on cloud-based solutions, but our government, a stone's throw from Silicon Valley, couldn't muster the technology for basic service. Millions of Californians were paying the price: come Christmas, food banks throughout the state were still overwhelmed.

With California having nearly the highest unemployment in the country combined with the slowest delivery of benefits, many people were wondering: What good is an unemployment office if it can't help you when you lose your job, especially when you've lost it on the government's orders? All the while, EDD was patting itself on the back. The agency put out regular press releases trumpeting how many claims it *had* processed (more than New York and Texas combined, one release boasted) and how many billions had been distributed—as if the agency were dispensing these funds in charity rather than returning them to the taxpayers who underwrite the system.

Newsom was also categorically excluding people from benefits in arbitrary ways. Californians who had mixed income, part W-2 and part 1099, were ineligible for benefits under the CARES Act because of an oversight. I asked the Governor to fill in this gap, in the same way he'd set aside $75 million for undocumented immigrants, who were also ineligible. He refused. The EDD also forced thousands of people who had made a mistake on their application to serve "penalty weeks," a kind of government-imposed timeout with no benefits. I wrote a letter signed by a bipartisan group of Legislators, and EDD actually agreed to change the policy, but in a roundabout way designed to deceive the federal government. Worst of all, as discussed in Chapter 6, independent contractors suffered long delays as Newsom, the EDD, and the Special Interests behind AB 5 plotted how best to exploit their sudden need to interface with the agency. Congressman Adam Schiff had to admonish his own Governor to stop holding back these benefits.

* * *

There was one group of claimants for whom the delivery of benefits was swift and seamless: California prisoners who were not entitled to them. On November 23, a group of nine local district attorneys, led by Sacramento County District Attorney Anne Marie Schubert, uncovered "the most significant fraud of taxpayer funds in California history." It might have been the most sensational story of government failure in recent memory, if our state had not provided so much competition already in 2020.

The district attorneys found that 35,000 fraudulent claims had been filed in the names of inmates, with 20,000 of them already paid. Bank of America would report that the fraud spanned 345,000 of its accounts. While other states had detected some fraud, the bank said "the scale of program fraud in California is unique." Stolen funds were already thought to be around $1 billion, though some estimates suggested the ultimate loss could be closer to $8.5 billion. "The practical reality is the vast majority of this money will never be repaid," El Dorado County District Attorney Vern Pierson said. The names used in the scheme included rapists, child molesters, and 133 Death Row inmates, including Scott Peterson and multiple serial killers. Among other "claimants" were Dianne Feinstein, John Doe, and Poopy Britches. The more we learned about this scandal, the worse it got: Tens of thousands of debit cards landed in states nowhere near California. Hundreds of cards would be sent to the same address, and some went directly to prisons. Benefits were issued to "infants or children as well as centenarians." Some fraudsters "even flout[ed] their illegal windfalls" in YouTube videos. "Undoubtedly, this money has been utilized to fund further criminal conduct," the prosecutors noted.

Assemblyman David Chiu, a Democrat from San Francisco, summed up the intolerable irony: "It's egregious that my constituents make a single typo that holds up their EDD benefits for months, while an inmate on death row can use a fake name and still get benefits paid out." The district attorneys also advised Newsom of the zero-sum reality: "Fraudulent unemployment claims deny those who have lost their employment, many due to COVID-19, who are legally eligible for benefits and are truly in need from getting the financial assistance they need."

The prosecutors did not hold back in identifying how this scheme was allowed to happen. According to the Sacramento Bee, "The district attorneys said neither the Employment Development Department nor Gov. Gavin Newsom have done enough to try to stop the fraudulent payments," which were ongoing. "We have asked and implored the governor to turn the spigot off," said Sacramento District Attorney Schubert, a registered Independent. EDD was not cross-checking claims with prison rolls as the vast majority of states were and as the federal government had advised, making the scheme "relatively easy" in Schubert's assessment. Schubert called EDD's response "slow and nonexistent," and advised Newsom to "look to other states for solutions." Fresno County District Attorney Lisa A. Smittcamp said Newsom "did nothing until the elected district attorneys brought it to the media," adding she did not think the state "has a handle on it." Riverside County District Attorney Michael Hestrin had a similar takeaway: "I don't know who was at the wheel."

Yet Newsom responded to the largest taxpayer fraud in history—which had occurred on his watch and was keeping benefits out of the hands of Californians who were jobless because of his own orders—by trying to defend himself. In a letter to the district attorneys, "Newsom pushed back on suggestions that he dragged his feet, saying the state took steps as early as September to 'deter and eliminate fraudulent claims.'" Reported the Bee: "He didn't elaborate on those steps." Newsom also floated the creation of another task force, prompting a barbed response from Democrat Assemblywoman Cottie Petrie-Norris. "We do not need a task force to implement simple and obvious steps that are implemented across the country," she said. "It's absurd. This is outrageous."

The "Data Glitch"

Government performance failures were not limited to the EDD. They were repeatedly compromising California's pandemic response and reopening plans.

On Monday, August 3, Newsom admitted the state's COVID case data had been wrong for weeks because of a major "glitch." The Governor, who had been holding press conferences almost every day, then disappeared from public view for a week. The Associated Press reported, "Newsom's office did not respond Friday to questions about why he was not personally holding one of his frequent daily briefings to explain and account for problems with the CalREDIE data." In Newsom's absence, Health and Human Services Secretary Mark Ghaly was charged with addressing the matter: "We apologize. You deserve better," he said.

According to Ghaly, the problem began with a "computer server outage" but was "compounded by the state's failure to renew a 2-year-old certificate for one of the nation's largest commercial labs, meaning the state did not receive updates for five days from Quest Diagnostics." The result, per the AP, was that "county health officials say they've been flying blind, unable to conduct robust contact tracing or monitor health factors without timely information, especially at a time when parents are on edge about school plans." The upshot was that while Californians had been told to put their lives on hold in deference to "data," we were learning that because of the Administration's negligence, the data was wrong. The LA Times also reported the Administration became aware of the issue "days before" Newsom cited the erroneous data to the public.

Six days after the revelation we still had not heard from the Governor. But late that Sunday night, his Director of Public Health, Dr. Sonia Angell, abruptly resigned. No reason was given. When Newsom finally emerged the next day, it was perhaps the worst display of obfuscation and accountability dodging of any press conference in the COVID era. When asked about Dr. Angell's departure, Newsom flatly refused to say whether she had resigned at his request or to explain it at all, calling it a "personnel matter" as though he were referring to an employee of his PlumpJack winery. Several reporters were not satisfied with this. A reporter for the Associated Press pointed out that Angell was "a State top public health officer" so there was a "public interest in why she left." Newsom still refused to answer, saying "the decision was made."

I called for an investigation and oversight hearing, but Newsom had another idea: a self-investigation. This became a favorite trick, to consume the entire field of inquiry with an internal investigation so there was no room for the Legislature, Auditor or any independent authority to seek out real answers. Later in the month when rolling blackouts by PG&E affected large parts of the state, Newsom assured the public: "We've got an investigation moving forward, and in real time, we'll let you and others know what we determine. I am not pleased with what's happened. We'll get to the bottom of it." In a letter to his own hand-picked political appointees directing the investigation, he claimed he was "not informed until moments before the blackouts started." As noted in Chapter 2, Newsom had actually approved the blackout plan and, while lambasting PG&E's "corporate greed," was the utility's single largest beneficiary of political funding.

As to the data glitch, the Legislature eventually got around to holding a limited hearing several weeks later. Newsom officials testified they failed to anticipate the COVID data "glitch" because they didn't expect a ten-fold increase in case data. I asked the Chief Information Officer how this could be when Newsom famously projected 26 million California cases. His response: "I'm not sure, I can't really answer it." I also asked the Chief Deputy Public Health Director why Newsom himself presented false COVID data to the public even after the Administration knew about the data glitch. "That is one of the quality control issues we have put back in place," I was told.

* * *

Any Californian who had ever been to the DMV was aware, well before COVID-19, of the infuriating gap between what we pay for as taxpayers and the quality of service we get in return. Likewise, anyone in the field will tell you that California's unemployment system has long been the worst in the country. Gavin Newsom cannot be blamed for inheriting a massive bureaucracy that was archaic, rigid, and in the thrall of Special Interests.

But in 2020, we needed to do better. We needed our government to become more modern, performance-based, and at the service of Californians. That required leadership, which Newsom had every opportunity and extraordinary power to provide. Instead, he reinforced the bureaucracy's worst qualities: using state agencies not just to respond to the pandemic but to advance his political priorities, dodging accountability in every way he could, failing to guide the machinery of government through the storm. The executive branch was left rudderless, with awesome power but limited capability—woefully ill-equipped to meet the challenges of the COVID era. It was a political failure of astonishing proportions.

On December 30, 2020, as he appointed a new Director of the EDD, Newsom vaguely alluded to the debacle of the preceding year: "California has certainly not escaped this national crisis unscathed," he said. After all of the harm caused by his government's incompetence, he could only acknowledge it as some minor by-product of a "national crisis" outside his control. With the new year a day away, Newsom demonstrated one final time, as he had throughout 2020, that he's simply unwilling to accept responsibility. In 2021, Californians can see to it that he never has to take responsibility for anything again.

CHAPTER NINE

Partisan

"Good morning. The GOP have now lost the popular vote in 7 of the last 8 presidential elections." – Gavin Newsom, Nov. 5, 2020

The deaths of Iranian terrorist Qasem Soleimani and Supreme Court Justice Ruther Bader Ginsburg were among the most notable of 2020. Naturally, they evoked very different reactions from the American public. But one American, Gavin Newsom, responded to the two events in exactly the same way.

As we woke to the news of Soleimani's killing on January 3, Newsom tweeted, "Today is a good day to remind ourselves that elections matter. Vote." Shortly after news broke of Ginsburg's passing, Newsom posted a brief tribute, then a mere four minutes later followed up with a one-word tweet: "VOTE." Such commands from Newsom were a steady drumbeat throughout the year. On October 24, he tweeted:

"VOTE. VOTE."

Often, of course, Newsom had thoughts on *who* to vote for. His tweets were sprinkled with phrases like, "It's time to vote them out." On November 1, California's Governor even had a recommendation for the voters of South Carolina as their Senator Lindsay Graham faced reelection. "Vote this deranged man OUT of office," Newsom tweeted.

As his Mario Kart animation had made clear with its red and blue characters, Newsom's approach to politics was one rooted in division. He used social media to engage in partisan warfare and mirrored that modus operandi in his words and deeds as a first-year Governor. At times it seemed his main constituency was not the Californians of diverse political views he was entrusted to lead, but the national activists and opinion leaders who held his ticket onto a bigger stage.

These were exactly the wrong qualities for a governor in the COVID era. In responding to the pandemic, Newsom's partisan zeal was not merely a distraction but an ever-present obstacle. He exploited the crisis for political ends, seeded public health guidance with fodder for partisan appetites, and tribally divided Californians at a time when unity was more needed than ever.

America's Most Partisan Governor

Newsom had a particular obsession with Mitch McConnell. In the second half of 2019, he had tweeted about the U.S. Senate Majority Leader 27 times, with statements like "@senatemajldr and @realDonaldTrump—you sicken me," "@senatemajldr should be ashamed of himself," "The cowardice of @senatemajldr will have a lasting impact on generations to come," and "Hey, @senatemajldr: Kentucky has a Democratic Governor. Look out."

This obsession did not abate in the COVID era, with nine McConnell-related tweets in the last few months of 2020, including: "Mitch McConnell once again puts his own self interests and desire for power above the needs of the American people," "Mitch McConnell's soulless inaction and willingness to put the lives and livelihoods of millions of Americans on the line for his own political gain is simply disgusting," and "Let's put Mitch McConnell out of a job." One Newsom tweet even gave a definition of invertebrates as including "well known animals such as jellyfish, corals, slugs, snails, octopuses, and Mitch McConnell."

Newsom's unrestrained partisanship went a step further on October 12, 2020 when he declared: "Nothing reeks of desperation quite like the Republican Party organization these days – willing to lie, cheat, and threaten our democracy all for the sake of gaining power." This was a reference to ballot collection boxes made available to the public by the state Republican Party, which Newsom called illegal; a Sacramento judge would rule to the contrary in what the LA Times called "a significant victory for GOP officials who have insisted their ballot collection campaign is following state election law." At the same time, California's Secretary of State, Alex Padilla, had awarded a $35 million COVID-related "voter education" contract to a partisan PR firm that worked for the Biden Campaign and California congressional candidates. State Controller Betty Yee, a Democrat, found the no-bid contract to be illegal and stopped payment, yet the ads were still made and aired. A Sacramento Bee editorial called it a "questionable politicization of the voting process," concluding that the "partisan-tinged scandal" had "tarnish[ed] our election system." But Newsom did not accuse Padilla of scheming to "lie, cheat, and threaten our democracy." He appointed him to the United States Senate.

As was to be expected, given his "VOTE" tweet launched moments after Justice Ginsburg's death, Newsom threw himself into the Supreme Court confirmation battle with gusto—even though it had nothing to do with his job and there was plenty to attend to in California. He quickly started trolling the likes of Lindsay Graham, Mitch McConnell, and Amy Coney Barrett herself. Newsom posted a "gotcha" video of Barrett supposedly supporting his view of whether an appointment was appropriate so close to an election. In fact, the video was fake news, having been manipulated to remove the context making it clear that was not the point she was making at all. Newsom was eventually forced to delete the tweet, though he never apologized to Barrett or corrected the record for the millions of people who saw it, and he would continue to demean Barrett with misleading attacks during the confirmation hearings.

Partisanship Gone Viral

In March 2020, Newsom raised eyebrows with some borderline complimentary statements about the President. But the reality was he was using partisanship to dismiss criticism of his policies from the beginning. In an April 3 appearance on the View, Newsom was asked about Congressman Devin Nunes's suggestion that schools did not need to close indefinitely. Newsom retorted: "I don't want to give him much air. I have not sourced him for advice on pretty much any issue and I say that as respectfully as I can." Newsom said he would "try to avoid some elected officials who frankly may not have the benefit of some of the insight that many of us do here." Shortly thereafter, as we have seen, Newsom tapped the nation's all-time biggest partisan mega-donor, fresh off the presidential campaign trail, not only for advice but to head California's economic recovery.

As the COVID era wore on, Newsom would link partisanship and the virus unlike any other Governor. On October 24 he released a spurious chart ranking "red" and "blue" states by COVID cases. Taken as a screenshot from a website called "Dan's COVID Charts," there were many problems with the chart's presentation: it ignored confounding variables, it cut cases off at June and cut the states off after 25, and it ignored data for deaths and hospitalizations. Even taking the measure at face value, however, the trend was ironically the exact opposite for counties within California at the time. And now, in early January, California has itself been leading the nation in new cases. So much for Newsom's football-spiking comment when he released the chart: "We're keeping Californians alive and healthy."

Even if the chart did convey something meaningful, it is hard to see what purpose could possibly be served by posting it. If the Governor wanted to make some point about the efficacy of particular COVID interventions, he could have done so without adding partisanship to the mix. That would certainly have been a better way to persuade people than condemning an entire party with which millions of his constituents affiliated. In truth, there was a diversity of approaches among states, irrespective of party, as there was a great diversity of opinion among the population that did not neatly break down along partisan lines. While the chart revealed nothing useful about the virus, it did illustrate priorities of the Governor's that were far removed from the health of Californians and of our body politic.

Adding further clarity to those priorities was Newsom's stated intention to use COVID-19 to "reshape the way we do business and how we govern" as part of "reimagining a new progressive era as it relates to capitalism." He reiterated this sentiment on CNBC on May 19, saying COVID would require everyone to become "more capable of meeting a regulatory mindset." Public opinion polls were clear that Californians believed the state's priority needed to be defeating the virus—not undertaking a project of political transformation—yet Newsom was consistently sending signals about the latter to a national audience.

In California, those signals were being translated into policy by diktat. At our October trial, we pointed out that 24 of Newsom's Executive Orders relied on unrestricted "police powers" purportedly granted by Section 8627 of the Emergency Services Act. Newsom's lawyers could not identify a single Executive Order any other Governor in 50 years of the Act's history had ever issued pursuant to that provision. Yet Newsom used it to create new policy without limit, issuing orders that touched on many "progressive" goals—an eviction moratorium, price controls, workplace liability rules, vote-by-mail, paid sick leave, debt collection, prisoner re-entry, and others. Some of these would have been unobjectionable as properly enacted temporary measures. But there was an unavoidable suspicion that their unlawful COVID-era adoption would be used to propel permanent policy changes—which in some cases has already come to pass.

Newsom's partisanship affected not just the content of his "emergency" policies and the lawless means of their enactment, but also the way he carried them out. The vote-by-mail order, for example, was steeped in grandiose statements about not having to choose between one's life and one's vote, with other states chided for forcing that choice upon their unsuspecting citizens. The Steyer Commission was billed not just as an economic recovery task force but as a vehicle for far-reaching political objectives. As will be discussed in the next chapter, Newsom communicated public health measures like wearing a mask in the most divisive and condescending of ways, seemingly designed more for consumption by the Twitter-verse than observance by Californians. Even where this was not the case, Newsom's continual partisan warfare had undercut his credibility: If he was willing to post fake news about Amy Coney Barret for a few retweets, how could he be a trusted source of authority for all Californians?

On November 7, Joe Biden did what leaders often do after an election and tried to bring the country together. "I will be a President for all Americans—whether you voted for me or not," he said. Gavin Newsom had a different reaction: "Good morning. The @GOP have now lost the popular vote in 7 of the last 8 presidential elections."

* * *

In my March 16 speech to the Assembly, I said "the partisan rituals of ordinary politics have no place in these extraordinary times." Gavin Newsom did not get the message. Instead, he made the politicization of COVID a ritual in itself, using the crisis to bolster his bona fides as a partisan warrior.

Now that he faces a recall, Newsom has already made it clear that partisan warfare will be his defense. His campaign has repeatedly described the Recall as driven by "Trump supporters," saying "the Trump train doesn't want to leave the station." Newsom's political mentor, Willie Brown, previewed this strategy in a December 19 column (which was back up and running after Newsom created the exception to AB 5 for him). "He has to paint the recall effort as an attack by disgruntled supporters of President Trump," Brown wrote. "If Newsom can make it about Trump, Newsom wins."

In truth, Californians of all parties are supporting the Recall, because the betrayals of public trust outlined in this book are not of a partisan nature. A recall is an inherently confrontational event. But by breaking free of America's most divisive Governor, I believe we can come together again as a state.

CHAPTER TEN

Hypocritical

"Don't be selfish." – Gavin Newsom

When Utah Governor Gary Herbert announced a statewide mask mandate, he explained the policy to Utahns in a televised address. "Masks do not negatively affect our economy, and wearing them is the easiest way to slow the spread of the virus," he said. "Individual freedom is certainly important, and it is our rule of law that protects that freedom. Laws are put in places to protect all of us. That's why we have traffic lights, speed limits and seatbelts, and that's why we now have a mask mandate."

One might quibble with Governor Herbert's analogies, and the new policy was certainly met with opposition. But it was a very different tone than California's Governor took when he announced a similar mandate in June of 2020. "Simply put, we are seeing too many people with faces uncovered," Newsom reproached the public. He then tweeted, "Don't be selfish. Wear a mask." Seeing this get traction on the social media platform, he tweeted it again: "Don't be selfish – Wear a mask."

Newsom had not mentioned mask-wearing in a single tweet before announcing the mandate—even though some states, like Rhode Island, had been requiring them for over a month. But as soon as his first tweet on the subject did well, it became fodder for relentless sloganeering along the lines of his VOTE series. "WEAR A MASK" and "WEAR

YOUR MASK" and "WEAR. A. MASK" were tweeted 17 different times. Lowercase versions appeared in several dozen more tweets, along with variations like "Be kind. Wear a mask," "Be smart. Wear a mask," and a dithyramb about masking-wearing as "a sign of toughness...a sign of someone who gives a damn," which Newsom called "a beautiful thing." Finally, there was, "Me again: You really need to wear a mask," with the *reallys* arrayed vertically.

Then came the French Laundry.

Do As I Say

If Newsom's only sin were disobeying his own orders, then the restaurant's name probably would not have so quickly entered the global lexicon as synonymous with lockdown hypocrisy. The Governor had not just issued edicts from on high, but in pursuit of COVID superstardom, had turned them into a character test—then failed the test himself in the most spectacular of ways.

The French Laundry is "one of the world's most exclusive restaurants." Its building in Napa Valley dates to 1900 and is on the National Registry of Historic Places. It is routinely on the list of the Top 50 Restaurants of the World put out by Restaurant Magazine and is one of only 14 three-Michelin-star restaurants in the United States. The owner, Thomas Keller, won the award for Best California Chef in 1996 and the Best Chef in America in 1997. Guests can pick between two nine-course tasting menus, neither of which uses the same ingredient twice. The food is French with "contemporary American influences." After Newsom's infamous dinner, the Onion ran a satirical article about how he was criticized "for eating at The French Laundry when Atelier Crenn offers a clearly superior take on contemporary cuisine."

The November 6 gathering that attracted the Governor was a 50th birthday celebration for one of the Capitol's most powerful lobbyists. Several other lobbyists were in attendance, including two from the California Medical Association. Photographs would show that the guests sat closely together and did not wear masks. The table appeared to be indoors. The wine bill alone was reported at $12,000, and there was a "careless, Gatsby-esque vibe" with other patrons complaining about the noise. The event took place just as the Governor was about to impose new "emergency brake" restrictions across California, followed shortly by a curfew and then a new stay-at-home order.

When the story broke a week later, the reaction was immediate. It took off on social media, and before long just about the whole state knew what had happened. The New York Times, whose coverage Newsom coveted, ran a story headlined "For California Governor the Coronavirus Message Is Do as I Say, Not as I Dine." The Sacramento Bee editorialized the next day that nothing could "launder the stain of stupidity from" Newsom's "reputation after this ill-conceived outing."

The Bee editorial unpacked the "layers of bad judgment," noting first that "it's no secret that the Newsoms have tons of money, but it's très gauche of them to flaunt it at a time like this." Next the editorial highlighted the terrible optics of feting a "Newsom insider and lobbying firm partner with a knack for getting his way in the corridors of power." Finally, it pointed to the "stunning hypocrisy," as Newsom "eschewed state public health guidelines to dine with friends at a time when the governor has asked families to scale back Thanksgiving plans." The Bee Editorial Board, which had endorsed Newsom in his run for governor, concluded: "Two years into his first term, and nine months into the COVID-19 pandemic, Newsom still can't get his act together. If Newsom can't get his head into the game, perhaps he should make this governor thing a one-term affair and leave the job open for someone with a desire to lead."

Newsom compounded his problems with dishonesty. At his next press conference, he "told reporters the party was outside where the coronavirus is less likely to spread," but within days photos surfaced showing "a private dining room that looked mostly inside." While Newsom claimed he "took safety precautions," the photos showed otherwise; there was no social distancing and no masks, even when guests were standing up mingling away from the table. In any case, according to a guidance put out by the Governor's Office earlier in the year, masks should have been worn *between bites* even during the nine-course meal.

At this time, millions of Californians remained unemployed. Their lives had been upended by orders of the Governor that he refused to justify with evidence. Many were struggling desperately to provide for their families as they'd waited months for checks owed to them by Newsom's EDD office; they'd soon learn those checks were often going to hardened prisoners able to exploit the Governor's negligent management. All the while, Newsom presumed to control almost every facet of their lives and called them selfish for not doing as he said. Now, here he was enjoying a world-class dining experience beyond their wildest imaginings. As he reveled in the company of the lobbyists who funded his campaigns, controlled our Capitol, and made it so hard for many people to get by even in good times, Newsom flouted his own diktats in precisely the way he'd denounced as "not giving a damn."

In truth, Newsom had never seemed to appreciate the impact of his actions on people's lives, or perhaps just hadn't cared. This was the case with AB 5, when he notoriously said, "I'm not sure those jobs were killed," and it had been the case throughout the COVID-19 era. Even in March, when he first issued the stay-at-home order, Newsom released an animation showing which establishments had to close. After depicting open supermarkets and other "essential" businesses, it showed several small businesses like salons and restaurants operating as normal until suddenly the people inside literally just go up in smoke. This was not an opponent of the policy dramatizing its effect; it was the Governor's own public service announcement.

Several months before the French Laundry dinner, cases were beginning to rise. Tom Steyer, for his part, said it was not the "people's fault." He explained that "if there was a mistake made, it was in not preparing people to understand that opening up with protocols was possible, but that those protocols were critical to the state working." For Newsom, on the other hand, the blame lay squarely with Californians. "We cannot continue to do what we have done over the last number of weeks," he warned. "It is our behaviors that are leading to these numbers." The Governor went on to say that "some have developed a little amnesia. Others have just, frankly, taken down their guard," adding that "the reality is people are mixing, and that is increasing the spread of this virus." Newsom even asked, "If you cannot practice physical distancing, then are you practicing love?"

Lashing out at the people of California not only betrayed a misanthropic bent, but ignored their heroic efforts for weeks on end to successfully "flatten the curve." Californians were willing to make sacrifices for the common good—cell phone data showed they stayed home when it was asked of them—but they were not willing to make pointless sacrifices that the Governor failed to justify and refused to make himself.

Capitol Hypocrisy

In the words of Rob Stutzman, a veteran political strategist who frequently supplies sound bites to the media, the French Laundry scandal "plays on all the things people imagine are the worst things about politics—and it turns out to be true." This is half-right. The reality of politics in California is actually even worse than most people imagine.

It is certainly worse than I imagined when I first became a legislator. Aside from internships growing up, I had never worked in politics. But I had seen the disastrous consequences of our state's misgovernance on education, economic opportunity, public safety, and our overall quality of life. I ran for office precisely because I believed our government was failing—but still, it was worse than I imagined. I discovered our state's political class had perfected a sham legislative process that is designed to maximize value for the Special Interests who control entry into that class. I saw how richly those interests had flourished while California became a state with more poverty, inequality, and homelessness than anywhere—a state that is literally deteriorating, a state where over half the population wants out, a state where two-thirds believe the American Dream is dead.

Politicians, by and large, did not feel the effects of this decline. They had a reliable paycheck and a generous per diem. They created a special DMV only for themselves. They attended plush fundraisers and receptions every night of the week in Sacramento. They went on all-expenses-paid junkets at the most alluring destinations around the world. They put their kids in private school to escape the failed public education system they were responsible for—just as Newsom sent his kids to in-person private school while his lockdown orders kept millions of less fortunate families struggling with remote learning.

Newsom's French Laundry outing put this disconnect on vivid display. In a New York Times column subtitled, "A lavish dinner helped reinforce the idea that California's government is a mess of bureaucratic dysfunction and aristocratic indifference," Miriam Pawel described California government as the "bastion of an out-of-touch elite oblivious to people's needs." Newsom's dinner, she wrote, "dramatized the chasm that divides California—more severely than North versus South or inland versus the coast...It is hard to say which was more astounding, the hypocrisy or the hubris."

Both the hypocrisy and the hubris ran even deeper. California politicians not only let powerful interests run our state into the ground while escaping the consequences themselves, but at the same time claimed they were advancing "liberal" and "progressive" ideals in the name of "social justice." The leader of the State Assembly even claimed California was building a "utopia." This farce was what Edwin Lombard, CEO of the Black Chamber of Commerce, identified with clarity as Newsom and the Legislature stood by AB 5 in the thick of the COVID shutdown and even connived to reinforce it. He responded directly to the author of the bill, who had tried to prop up the corrupt law not only by claiming it was about "worker protection" but also by somehow connecting it to ongoing demonstrations around the use of force by police.

"Black lives, Black families and Black businesses have been devastated by the triple catastrophes of AB5, COVID-19, and the violent racism that permeates the very institutions we rely on to protect our freedom as Americans," he wrote. "How dare you use the shooting of civilians by police as a political weapon to defend your misguided and disastrous law that has robbed thousands of Californians of their right to earn a living with dignity, respect, and independence. The Black men and women who have chosen to work for themselves are not asking for your 'protection' from self-employment. We are not asking for your permission to earn a living as we choose, by starting a business for ourselves or control our own future as an independent contractor. We're tired of paternalistic institutions that purport to 'protect' us while enabling, defending, and propagating the systemic racism that has cost so many Black lives. AB 5 has already crushed thousands of Black businesses and will keep more from operating in the Gig Economy. Nearly a million Californians would lose jobs, opportunities, and independence if the future of AB 5 were up to you... We're not asking for your help or misguided protection. Just open the door and let us help ourselves."

* * *

After reading that statement on the Floor of the Assembly in June 2020, I addressed my colleagues: "I see California's political leadership, including the Governor and Members of this Assembly, speak in high tones about issues of social justice," I said. "But all it takes is a phone call from a big enough Special Interest and you'll turn your back on any community."

In a break from decorum, the author of the bill and the Chair of the Labor Committee had just attacked me personally on the Assembly Floor for trying to repeal the bill, so I turned to their remarks. "When I hear these repeated cheap shots and personal attacks I just don't engage with it at all—because I know that you guys, in particular, aren't the problem. The problem is we have a Legislature that isn't run by Legislators." I paused, then concluded: "But we all have the capacity to change that. We all have the ability to start governing in the public interest. On this bill right now, we could consciously decide not just to award freedom in small doses but to start treating all Californians with the dignity and respect they deserve." Of course, the Legislature did not change anything. And the Governor did not change anything, except to make our politics an order of magnitude worse.

So now it's up to us, the people of California, to exercise our sovereign power and give full expression to that timeless phrase from the Declaration of Independence: "the consent of the governed." I believe if this Recall succeeds, it can inaugurate not just a new Governor but a new paradigm for our public life, where hypocrisy gives way to integrity, where corruption is overcome by decency, where our state's steady decline—now a freefall—is swiftly reversed and a new era for the California Dream begins.

CHAPTER ELEVEN

Neglectful

"We're going to be dusting that off." – Gavin Newsom, referring to his moribund Health Corps on Nov. 30, 2020

Gavin Newsom, master of the novel coronavirus, took to CNN for a victory lap on April 1, 2020. Ticking off the keys to his pandemic response, Newsom delivered the epidemiological verdict: "While we see things increasing, we don't see them increasing as fast as other parts of the country," he told Jake Tapper.

Having tamed the virus at home, the Governor could turn his attention to those less enlightened states that had yet to do everything California had. "My message is this, what are you waiting for? What more evidence do you need...Don't dream of regretting, lean into the moment, take responsibility. Meet it head on. You'll never regret overcompensating at the moment so that you're preparing people for meeting this moment in the responsible way."

Even at this *moment*, CNN's Tapper perhaps sensed he was being taken on a tour of a Potemkin village. "The CDC says that your state, California, has a testing backlog of nearly 60,000 tests," he noted. "What's being done about that?" From Newsom's long-winded answer, it was clear to anyone watching that there really was no answer. In fact, nearly every facet of California's direct public health response apart from the one Newsom seemed to relish—restricting human activity—was lagging behind the rest of the nation. Worst among these failures,

Newsom would squander the talents and goodwill of tens of thousands of California healthcare professionals who could have helped stave off the nation's worst COVID-19 surge.

The Vanishing California Health Corps

On March 30, Governor Newsom announced a "a major new initiative to staff at least an additional 50,000 hospital beds needed for the COVID-19 surge." He unveiled the California Health Corps, where doctors, nurses, and a variety of other healthcare professionals, who were either recently retired, still in school, or for some other reason not part of the workforce, were "encouraged to step up and meet this moment to help California respond to the outbreak." I thought it was a great idea. It was a way to bolster our healthcare capacity, prepare for any surge, and tap into a civic spirit brimming across the state.

Newsom estimated the Health Corps would "increase our ranks by another 37,000-plus" workers who would be "distributed throughout our healthcare delivery system." They would "provide for the kind of human capital surge that we'll need to meet the moment." On April 7, Newsom revealed the initial results, which were impressive: "81,879 people have filled out a formal application," he said. "That will provide the surge capacity in terms of personnel we'll need to appropriately staff" additional hospital beds. The total applications would eventually surpass 94,000. When Newsom announced the signups, it made me proud of our state. Imagine what would be possible, I thought, if we could find ways to come together like this for a civic purpose more often. The Governor was right when he said, "California's health care workers are the heroes of this moment."

On December 3, 2020 Newsom made a very different announcement. With cases surging in California, he announced a new stay-at-home order that was triggered by a single metric: ICU capacity. I heard from my local hospitals that the limiting factor for them was personnel shortages, and KCRW radio confirmed that when hospitals "say they're running out of capacity, they mean they're running out of staff." Thus, nine months into the pandemic, Californians were going to be confined to their homes because we did not have enough healthcare workers. Where was the Health Corps? It turned out that of the 94,000 people who signed up, 21 of them were currently deployed. Not twenty-one thousand. Twenty-one.

A December 8, 2020 story by KCRW radio put it this way: "Now seems to be the perfect time to deploy Newsom's 'Health Corps.' But hardly any of the 90,000 who signed up are available to help. Only a few hundred doctors and nurses are available. So what happened?" What happened was typical of California's COVID-19 experience. Newsom had gotten his headline when he announced the "major initiative" of the Health Corps and the gaudy signup numbers. After that, the initiative fizzled. Once again, Californians had stepped up and the Governor let them down.

* * *

On December 1, the Sacramento Bee published an investigative report headlined "Newsom asked California doctors and nurses to join his Health Corps. Why the plan flopped." The Bee had made a Public Records Act request and received deployment documents, showing that "dozens of hospitals and nursing homes had requested Health Corps resources but received no help from the group or fewer people than they had requested." Stephanie Roberson of the California Nurses Association, usually a stanch Newsom ally, said there had been "no progress whatsoever" on the Health Corps. When the Los Angeles Times asked why only 21 Health Corps members were deployed after the program "launched to great fanfare in the spring," a public health department spokesperson responded that "the agency is looking for ways to optimize the use of the volunteer program."

In the early days, a few applicants were indeed hired and deployed. But many of them "stood by at mostly empty 'surge' facilities, including the Sleep Train Arena in Sacramento, while some hospitals and nursing homes went without the qualified Health Corps workers they had requested." Doctors at Sleep Train clocked in for a couple weeks, saw barely any patients, then the facility was closed and they went home. When some of them reached out in December to ask if they were needed, they were told they would not be called back, and if they really wanted to help they had to submit a new application to join a whole different program. Some other Health Corps members said haphazard scheduling and training "made it difficult to stick with the program." Others were never able to be of service because they "were at the mercy of a confusing technology system that hampered deployments."

But most applicants never heard from the state at all. Assemblyman James Gallagher posted "CA Health Corps stories" from his constituents. Katrina from Corona said, "I signed up when it first came out, never heard a thing." Nikki from Alta explained, "I was one of those nurses who volunteered. I never got deployed. It keeps saying I'm in step 3 of 5 and to be ready to deploy. That's as far as it will let me go. Everything checked out but it's just stuck in the system." Brian from Paradise said, "Still waiting on my CNA license 9 months later still waiting on the state." Catherine from Stanislaus: "I was one that applied and never got any response. Ever." Priscilla from Yuba City: "I applied for this and haven't had anyone contact me yet at all."

The main issue, the Governor's Office asserted, was that most people who applied were ineligible. But it was Newsom who had predicted a 37,000-person boost to the workforce. Moreover, it was the state itself that was setting eligibility requirements, and some barriers—like AB 5, certain staffing ratios, and limits on final-semester nursing students, which California kept in place weeks after other states—were arbitrary or protectionist. There was also no apparent effort made to contact ineligible applicants to see if they had useful skillsets.

Yet on November 30, 2020, Newsom "renewed calls for healthcare workers to join Health Corps," saying, "We're going to be dusting that off." Rather than activating, maintaining, and nurturing this extraordinary pool of Californians willing to serve, so that they would be ready if the time came, the Governor had let the program gather dust on the shelf. When the time did come and personnel shortages became pressing, it was of little use. It was on the basis of that failure that Newsom shut down the state.

The Testing Mess

The testing backlog identified in Jake Tapper's interview with Newsom was not an anomaly. On April 20, an Associated Press analysis of data gathered by the COVID Tracking Project showed that California had the third-lowest testing rate in the country. Stephen Morrison, senior vice president at the Center for Strategic and International Studies, called this "puzzling" since California's mayors, along with Newsom, had been quicker than other states to pull the trigger on stay-at-home orders. Apparently testing was less of a priority, even though this was universally recognized by public health experts as crucial to containment of the virus.

I tried to bring this to Newsom's attention, saying in mid-April that while I had up to that point withheld criticism of him on testing, "We are undeniably in worse shape than almost any state." Newsom offered a "task force" to address the matter, but the situation did not improve. On July 15 leaders of three major healthcare associations released a statement warning that testing materials continued "to be in short supply" and urging Newsom "to commit state resources to immediately expand" their supply. Adding to the scarcity, Newsom would not allow pharmacies to conduct tests—perhaps at the behest of powerful medical interests—thus forgoing 6,300 testing sites spanning nearly every community in the state. Even when pharmacies were given a green light of sorts, it did little to improve overall capacity as it was only for swab-and-send tests, not the point-of-care tests with immediate results. The latter would not be authorized until late August.

Nate Silver, whose 538 website was collecting and analyzing testing data from every state, identified the consequences of California's meager testing regime: "a 6-to-1 ratio of infections to detected cases in Geneva and a 30-to-1 ratio in California might actually mean basically the same thing, given the high rate of testing in Geneva and the low rate in CA." On April 22, he noted that New York had done four times more tests per capita than California, adding, "California's testing situation is poor...and that should probably figure into some of the narratives that are praising leaders over there for their response." Silver vented about the reliability of California's data, saying that "California has some of the worst data in the country." He said that even if the testing picture were improving, "the state's data is such a mess that I'm not sure we'd really know." There were "substantial lags in reporting," and California was "perhaps the worst offender" in reporting negative tests "erratically."

In the view of some experts, this neglect had a considerable cost. While Californians had made enormous sacrifices by staying home for weeks, inadequate testing was one reason contact tracing was not sufficiently developed to keep infection rates down. Dr. Lee Riley, an infectious diseases professor at the University of California at Berkeley, said that "while the state managed to flatten the curve of rising cases, it never effectively bent the curve downward to the point infections would die out." That was because the state "was never able to do enough contact tracing to isolate infected people and those they may have exposed before they spread the disease."

* * *

At the time of this writing, in early January 2021, history appears to be repeating itself with distribution of the vaccine. California was lagging behind the national average as far as the percent of its allotted doses that had been administered.

On January 5, Newsom acknowledged the vaccine rollout was "too slow," yet "provided no clear answer during a news conference to questions about the cause of the lag, only promising 'a much more aggressive posture' and additional details in the coming days." Dr. Mike Wasserman, the past president of the California Association for Long Term Care Medicine and a member of the Governor's own vaccine advisory committee, said "hundreds of thousands of COVID vaccines across the state are sitting in warehouses with the potential of being wasted." He added, "My worst nightmares have been coming true over the last few weeks."

Exposing the Vulnerable

As of early January 2021, 9,206 of the COVID-19 deaths in California were at nursing homes, over a third of the state's total. Part of the cause was the inadequacy of the state's testing. "To keep the virus out of a nursing home, you need to be able to test staff regularly, every time they come in for a shift," said Katie Smith Sloan, president and CEO of the nonprofit LeadingAge. In addition, nursing homes "are chronically short staffed," something the Health Corps could have helped with if it had not been abandoned.

The Newsom Administration also provoked outrage among

senior and disability advocates in the early stages of the pandemic, when it advised hospitals "to prioritize younger people with greater life expectancy for care during the coronavirus outbreak." These guidelines were criticized as "discriminatory," as they communicated "what the medical establishment and state government think about disabled people and older adults," Claudia Center, legal director for the Disability Rights Education & Defense Funds said. "We know what this means, and we remember, and it's hurtful." However, the LA Times reported that as "quietly as the guidelines were initially posted online, the document was removed."

Meanwhile, one type of facility fully under state control—state prisons—became a hotbed for COVID-19. A November 2020 New York Times column reported that California had "failed another vulnerable population with even less recourse, and less political clout: The virus has spread through all the state prisons; more than 19,000 inmates have been infected and more than 80 have died." In late May, the California Department of Corrections and Rehabilitation so badly botched the transfer of 121 inmates into San Quentin—with no testing, a crowded bus ride, and immediate intermingling—that 2,200 prisoners, over 75 percent of the population, contracted COVID-19 and 28 died from it at just this one prison. Thirty employees of the prison also contracted the virus, with one dying.

A California Court of Appeal found "deliberate indifference" to the inmates' health on the part of the state, calling the outbreak "the worst epidemiological disaster in California correctional history." Assemblyman Marc Levine, a Democrat from Marin County whose district includes San Quentin, was unsparing in his criticism of the Administration. Noting that he "spoke with the Governor" and other Administration officials early in the pandemic about protecting our prison population and staff, he called what ensued the "worst prison health screw up in state history," adding, "We did not meet this moment." In calling for accountability, Levine said, "Never has 'too little too late' been more true or cruel. Never has 'better late than never' been so morally repugnant." The Newsom Administration, for its part, "respectfully disagree[d] with the court's determination." A department spokeswoman said it had "taken extensive actions to respond to the COVID-19 pandemic."

While California prisoners did not deserve fraudulent unemployment benefits, they certainly did not deserve to get the virus either. Yet under Governor Newsom's watch, both were reaching the state's correctional facilities in alarming numbers.

* * *

Gavin Newsom is not sought-after on national television programs these days, but he continues to applaud himself for having the clairvoyance, in mid-March of 2020, to follow the lead of six Bay Area counties that had issued stay-at-home orders. Yet as he basked in the glow of that intervention and presumed to advise other states on their own policies, he was neglecting the core government tasks that would allow for prolonged containment of the virus and a sustainable economic recovery.

The result, as we ended 2020, was headlines like "California's coronavirus surge is worst in nation—by a big margin." In a sense, it's a more dramatic iteration of what Californians had become accustomed to as we paid the nation's highest taxes while driving over the deepest potholes: sacrificing the most and getting the least in return. Only a shock to the system will change that, and perhaps Gavin Newsom's one great contribution to the life of our state will be providing an occasion for just that.

PART III

AFTER NEWSOM

CHAPTER TWELVE

Back to Basics

"If the majority vote on the question is to recall, the officer is removed." – California Constitution, Article 2, Section 15(c)

It's a warm summer night, a Tuesday, in late July of 2021. Most Californians are in their homes, glued to their television sets or smart phones as they watch history unfold. Shortly after 8:00 PM, the results are clear. For just the third time since our nation's founding, a governor has been recalled from office. What comes next?

The Anti-Newsom Roadmap

Removing Gavin Newsom will not solve California's problems all at once. He exemplifies those problems, and he has done more to compound them than anyone might have thought possible in a span of two years. So the Recall will certainly stop further damage. But to have lasting meaning, the mandate from this extraordinary act of popular sovereignty must be channeled into fundamental changes to our political institutions and political culture.

This book does not endeavor to fully develop those fundamental reforms, nor should they be developed by any one person. But Gavin Newsom provides us a useful starting point. The eight qualities of Newson's failed COVID response discussed in the preceding chapters are something of a roadmap. They put everything that has gone wrong with our politics on such stark display that their repudiation can set us on the opposite road we need to travel, providing guideposts for the journey ahead.

Humility: The opposite of Newsom's self-promotional mode of governance is one of humility. This means humility not only in the conduct of the state's chief executive, but in the role of the government itself. It means remembering that every action we take has legitimacy only by the consent of the people we represent. Concretely, that means a more open and deliberative approach to governance. It means restoring power to local institutions that know their communities best.

Humility also means focusing earnestly on the core functions of government. I call this a "Back to Basics" approach. Miriam Pawel wrote in the New York Times that California needs "leadership more focused on nonglamorous but essential government functions. A strategy that looked to score runs by hitting single after single, rather than always swinging for elusive home runs. So far that leadership has been in short supply." As one example, that would mean fewer projects like the high-speed rail, instead attending to our core infrastructure: roads, highways, and bridges that are uncongested and drivable; dams, reservoirs, and levies that are robust and reliable; power plants, grids, and transmission lines that are safe and affordable; forests, parks, and open spaces that are healthy and breathable.

The Rule of Law: The opposite of Gavin Newsom's lawless mode of governance is one that respects the rule of law. That means recognizing that written words are binding on those in positions of power. From this comes the most basic form of freedom—freedom from the arbitrary dominion and control of another. It's what gives life to the audacious premise that we as citizens are not mere subjects of state power but authors of our own political reality.

Respecting the rule of law means recognizing both the California and U.S. Constitutions as constraints on what the Governor, the

Legislature, or any official can do. It means restoring a proper separation of powers, where the Governor's job is to implement laws passed by the Legislature. Churning out orders with the stroke of a pen is certainly easier than a legislative process. But our Founders made a deliberate choice that exercising the powers of government should not be easy. As the ultimate safeguard of liberty, they defined those powers as limited, distributed, checked, and balanced—precisely the opposite of California in 2020.

The Public Interest: The opposite of Gavin Newsom's corrupt mode of governance is one dedicated to the public interest. This requires defusing the power of the "Third House" lobbyists who largely control the first two houses, the Assembly and Senate, as well as this Governor in particular. The Third House—consisting of lobbyists for union conglomerates, industry associations, and major companies—accounts for the vast majority of political funding in California. For many Legislators, how to vote on a bill comes down to nothing more than which interests are for or against it. With the Governor and legislators focused so intently on appeasing lobbyists within a few square blocks of the Capitol, relatively little attention is left for 40 million people throughout the state who have to live with legislative outcomes.

Changing this dynamic can be difficult to do through campaign finance laws, but it is achievable through a cultural change at the Capitol. That was my goal in becoming the first 100 percent citizen-backed California Legislator by declining all contributions from the Third House. Ultimately, accepting Third House contributions needs to be stigmatized, and that can start with political leaders, like a new governor, refusing to support any candidate of either party who accepts them.

Accountability: The opposite of Gavin Newsom's unscientific mode of governance is one that is informed by facts and data and accountable for its outcomes. Just as Newsom's political interests led him to dismiss sound science in responding to COVID-19, so it is that facts, data, and evidence often count for little when it comes to policy decisions at our Capitol. Indeed, policymaking often proceeds in a willfully ignorant manner.

Homelessness is an especially unfortunate example. In 2019, 1,039 homeless people died on the streets of Los Angeles, and the state's overall homeless population was growing faster than the rest of the country combined. At the same time, we spent $2.7 billion more to address the problem over a two-year period. The nonpartisan Legislative Analyst warned more funds would "quickly dissipate" because there was no strategy, yet in early 2020 Newsom wanted to add $1.4 billion in additional spending. I proposed a full audit of where funding was going and what outcomes were being achieved, so that our spending would be informed by data about what would best help Californians transition out of homelessness or avoid it altogether. I was one vote away from getting the audit approved when Newsom pressured three legislators to "abstain." The Audit Committee Chairman actually tried to cancel the vote as the Governor's aides eyed him from the witness table.

Citizen Service: The opposite of Gavin Newsom's incompetent mode of governance is an approach based on customer service. This means a new paradigm for the provision of government services that is modern, performance-based, and geared towards helping Californians. Countless businesses every day carry out the sort of tasks that befuddle the likes of the DMV and EDD. The priorities of these agencies must be completely realigned.

With the human capital and technology we have available to us, there is no reason Californians should have to put up with substandard service. The Legislature and Governor can work together on a total overhaul of the state bureaucracy: focusing its mission, modernizing its technology, and bringing in new talent with clear performance benchmarks for every agency of government.

Transparency: The opposite of Gavin Newsom's hypocritical approach to governance is to make the actions of our elected officials transparent to the public. This starts with eliminating perks like the secret DMV office, so lawmakers have to feel the effects of their own policy decisions. It means rooting out the many undemocratic practices at our Capitol, like the denial of public access or rules where a bill can be killed without a vote so that legislators can claim they didn't oppose it.

It also means insisting on policy to match the rhetoric of equity and social justice. In that regard, what is needed perhaps most of all is comprehensive education reform. A true commitment to equity would involve looking to what has worked in other states to reduce achievement gaps and propel student achievement. The same goes for the cost of living in California, especially housing, which gets worse every year as a result of deliberate policy choices even as lawmakers claim they are addressing the problem.

Unity: The opposite of Gavin Newsom's partisan approach to governance is one based on bringing people together. This means focusing on governing California and not letting the currents of national politics distract us from the enormous challenges we face. It means an agenda that is non-ideological, rooted in principles of good government, and aimed at solving our state's fundamental problems—that's what the Back to Basics approach is about. It means setting a new tone for our public life where we have spirited and robust debates to hash out our differences, but where that debate rests on a foundation of common values and shared purpose.

Responsibility: The opposite of Gavin Newsom's neglectful approach to governance is one that is mindful of our responsibilities. That California had for years de-prioritized pandemic preparedness before 2020 is emblematic of a broader tendency towards myopic decision-making. The long-term consequences pile up, until they are not long-term anymore. As one example, California's massively underfunded public pension system is not just a theoretical problem; increased payments to CalPERS and CalSTRS are eating into the budgets of school districts, cities, and counties. As another example, no reforms were made to California's unstable tax structure, despite urgent warnings from Jerry Brown and others, and it led to a historic deficit in 2020. Satisfying immediate political demands has been the way of the Capitol for too long. California needs a new model of political leadership based on durable stewardship of the public interest.

* * *

If the Recall is successful, the new Governor would likely be sworn in sometime in early September, which is just before the Legislature is set to recess for the year. But the Governor could call a Special Session dedicated to instituting the Recall's call for fundamental change. This timing would be optimal, as voters would have an opportunity to weigh in again the following year and could affirm the new Governor's approach while bringing accountability to any legislators who did not catch on that the era of corruption was over and a new era of public service had begun.

The 2022 election, with the Governor running alongside a slate of candidates committed to good government, could cement the Recall's goals. It could assure that this extraordinary movement is not a self-contained event, not an ephemeral moment of activism, but becomes imprinted into the structure of California political life. That would set our state on a new course, with no limit as to what we could achieve. And it could set the stage for restoring the greatest gift of our Founders: government that is truly by the people.

CHAPTER THIRTEEN

The Revival of Self-Government

"No sooner do you set foot upon the American soil, than you are stunned by a kind of tumult...Everything is in motion around you; here, the people of one quarter of a town are met to decide upon the building of a church; there, the election of a representative is going on; a little further, the delegates of a district are posting to the town in order to consult upon some local improvements; or in another place the labourers of a village quit their ploughs to deliberate upon the project of a road or a public school. Meetings are called for the sole purpose of declaring their disapprobation of the line of conduct pursued by the Government; whilst in other assemblies the citizens salute the authorities of the day as the fathers of their country." –Alexis de Tocqueville, Democracy in America, 1835

In 2018, Silicon Valley venture capitalist Tim Draper offered a modest proposal: the end of California. His ballot initiative, Proposition 9, would have divided the state into three chunks, which was half as many as another fragmentation plan he'd proposed four years earlier. Draper, who had been involved with companies like Hotmail, Skype, Tesla, and, more controversially, Theranos, explained the impetus for his proposal: "I looked at this and thought: We really need to start fresh. We need a way for governments to be accountable. We need a way to empower the residents of the state." Stephen Colbert called it "a great new plan to make California whole again by breaking it apart."

Draper was not the first to propose such a scheme. Since California was granted statehood in 1850, there have been at least 220 efforts to split it up one way or another. Draper's proposal, like all of the others, of course went nowhere. But the recurrence of this idea across generations is more than a testament to the enduring popularity of pie in the sky. It emanates from a real and growing strain on our social fabric: a belief that our politics are not a match for our culture, and that such a vast and diverse state requires a greater diffusion of power and authority. California, after all, has not only more people than any state but a larger gross domestic product than all but four countries. Yet as our population and economy have grown, political control has become more centralized, not less—and during the COVID-19 State of Emergency, Gavin Newsom was able to fast-forward that trend to its logical endpoint: one-man rule from Sacramento.

Rejecting his one-man rule therefore presents an opportunity to reverse that trend. But it does not require fracturing the state. Over 170 years, California has forged an identity of historic significance, one that's been a driving force in the affairs of our nation and the world. Something irreplaceable would be lost if it were to vanish. So how do we pursue the germ of insight in Draper's plan while maintaining a distinctly Californian identity? Perhaps Gavin Newsom was on to something in his infamous Rachel Maddow appearance after all.

***

On Maddow's show, Newsom proclaimed California a "Nation State" as a way to puff himself up. But taking the concept seriously would suggest a more modest state government. Take two actual nations of comparable size: Canada and Spain, which both have around 40 million people. Each has a federalist structure, with regional governments known as provinces in Canada and autonomous communities in Spain.

These regional governments, covering populations in the millions or hundred thousands, are self-governing in many respects, with the central government handling matters of national concern.

If California had a similar regional model, the relationship between the state government and the different regions would resemble the relationship of the U.S. government to the states—that is, the California state government would be one of limited powers. It would have a discrete set of specific functions, on matters of truly statewide concern, with everything else devolved to smaller units of government. California already has something like this with our university system: the UCs and CSUs have a unifying brand and a central administration to provide some standardization and coordination of activities, but each campus has its own distinct identity and governance.

Proposing a new stratum of regional governments in California, akin to provinces or autonomous communities, probably verges on Draper-esque quixotism. But the main advantage can be realized within California's existing institutional structure: a state government with far fewer responsibilities and authority devolved to the level of government as close to the people as practical. The nuts and bolts of governing—education, roads, and the like—would no longer be handled by state authorities. Policy would be more aligned with the circumstances, interests, and values of those it affects. State bureaucracies could be thinned considerably and reformed in a more performance-based, service-oriented mold. The State Legislature could perhaps be part-time, and regional organizations, like the Sacramento Area Council of Governments, could take on a larger role.

In late 2020, I worked with other legislators in my region to form a faint model of something like this. We convened a Conference of North State Representatives, with 16 counties sending a delegate. The resulting "Healthy Communities Resolution," which rejected Newsom's one-man rule and his failed COVID management in favor of a more localized and data-based approach, was then passed by boards of supervisors where the people of each county could have direct input.

This leads to the prime virtue of decentralizing political authority: a greater measure of representation. California has by far the least representative legislature in the United States, with legislative districts that are several times more populous than the next closest state and larger than some small countries. Each senator represents roughly one million people and each assemblymember half a million. That means the elected officials who wield the most power over our lives are the ones who we are least likely to have access to or to know. This also means they are the least likely to govern with a concern for the public good, as it's the expense of campaigning in enormous districts that has allowed Special Interests to hijack the process. Reallocating power to elected officials who represent smaller constituencies would thus lead to more public-spirited representation while enhancing the political agency of each citizen.

* * *

So far, we've actually been looking at self-government through the wrong end of the telescope. It's in the real places where we live our lives—the neighborhoods, the schools, the workplaces, the centers for clubs and associations—that true self-government takes place. For our Founding Fathers, the lifeblood of republicanism was local communities.

This communitarian foundation was what most impressed Alexis de Tocqueville about American society in 1835: "In these States, it is not only a portion of the people which is busied with the amelioration of its social condition," he wrote in his celebrated work, *Democracy in America*, "but the whole community is engaged in the task." This meant the "cares of political life engross a most prominent place in the occupation of a citizen in the United States; and almost the only pleasure of which an American has any idea, is to take a part in the Government, and to discuss the part he has taken." Tocqueville saw this spirit of self-government everywhere he looked: "This feeling pervades the most trifling habits of life...Debating clubs are to a certain extent a substitute for theatrical entertainments...This ceaseless agitation which democratic government has introduced into the political world, influences all social intercourse."

Such political engagement, de Tocqueville observed, was part of an active, localized, and edifying understanding of citizenship. "The native of New England," he wrote, "takes part in every occurrence in the place; he practices the art of government in the small sphere within his reach; he accustoms himself to those forms without which liberty can only advance by revolutions; he imbibes their spirit; he acquires a taste for order, comprehends the balance of powers, and collects clear practical notions on the nature of his duties and the extent of his rights." And while there were still legislatures, their work was not a substitute for the role of each citizen: "The great political agitation of the American legislative bodies...is a mere episode of a sort of continuation of that universal movement which originates in the lowest classes of the people and extends successively to all the ranks of society."

Beyond escaping the shadow of British imperialism, freedom for the Founding generation was inseparable from political participation. They did not want to replace one form of monarchy with a new division between the ruler and that the ruled. What our Founders set in motion was truly government by the people, with echoes of antiquity; in Athens, citizenship was understood as "having a share in the social and political community." While the exclusion of whole categories of people, including women and African Americans, means we can never look upon these times with uncritical nostalgia, there are lessons for restoring self-government today—especially in the state that has drifted farthest from it.

California does have many institutions of local government: counties, cities, school districts, and a variety of special districts like water or park districts. But these usually fail to actualize self-government in any meaningful way. One reason we've already noted: as appendages of the state, their responsibilities, procedures, scope of authority, mandates, and other functions are limited and imposed from afar. What that often means in practice is they become bureaucratic entities controlled by compliance-driven staffs, with the public-facing elements of governance essentially pro forma. That's why moving away from a model of governance where power is centralized in Sacramento would give existing local institutions a greater capacity to serve as vehicles of self-government.

The other problem is a deeper one. Our public-school system is not preparing young people for the responsibilities of citizenship. Complaints about inadequate civics education often focus on a failure to recite basic facts, like a 2018 study showing only a small fraction of respondents could answer questions like "Why did the colonists fight the British?" But the real deficiency doesn't mainly relate to hard knowledge. It goes to the very meaning of citizenship, which has been steadily reduced since Tocqueville's day. A student today generally does not learn "clear practical notions on the nature of his duties" or how to "practice[] the art of government in the small sphere within his reach"—nor, all too often, does he or she gain the capacity for critical thinking and habits of service needed for meaningful engagement in community life.

Increasingly our education system produces just the opposite, with an accepted orthodoxy imposed on students as normatively unchallengeable. We see one consequence of this in the growing intolerance for freedom of speech. Especially on college campuses, the tendency is to shut down opposing ideas rather than engage with them in spirited debate. I tried to take a small step to address this, partnering with the University of California on bipartisan legislation to teach the history and value of the First Amendment and help students develop habits of thoughtful discussion and an openness to new ideas. But a true civics education isn't just an add-on to the curriculum, or a Cliff Notes guide to the Constitution. It's integrated into all facets of schooling so that preparation for citizenship is an underlying purpose of one's education.

One model of this approach is John Adams Academy, a public charter school in Roseville that explicitly teaches the "responsibilities that require all to be participatory citizens in this democratic republic of self-government." Students not only learn the principles from America's founding documents but are taught "to understand how they developed throughout history" and to "incorporate core American principles in their own lives and to promote them in their communities." There is an emphasis on virtue as "a voluntary outward obedience to principles of truth and moral law" and "the voluntary sacrifice or subjugation of personal wants for the greater good of the community." These virtues are "developed and expressed" through each student's membership in the school community itself. John Adams aims to produce "entrepreneurs, who by their very nature are thinkers, leaders, and statesmen, who know how to solve problems and improve the world around them."

What most young people today get, by contrast, is essentially a constant stream of tweets from Gavin Newsom: VOTE VOTE VOTE. This is as much a do-not-enter sign as it is a welcome mat. With voting inculcated as the end all and be all of civic participation, the implicit message is: vote, and I'll see you again in two years. Just as Newsom implored people to vote dozens of times without once inviting them to participate in government in any other way, our larger political culture has reduced each citizen's role to the single self-contained act of casting a ballot. While the franchise is the lynchpin of democracy, and its expansion has marked the most important form of progress in our history, it wasn't itself the great American innovation. Self-government was. And in California, that's slipped away.

* * *

This Recall can be a moment of restoration, reanimating our stale political institutions with traces of Tocqueville's America and renewing the meaning of We the People. Our state has veered far from the vision of the Founders, and we are coming off a year where it was lost altogether. But 2021 is a chance for a course correction.

A new year, a new decade, offers hope of a new beginning. In a way, the story of our state is a story of new beginnings. It's a story unlike any other. And the people of California can now write an imaginative next chapter.

HOW YOU CAN HELP

The official petition for the Recall is collecting signatures now. It takes 1.5 million by March 17, 2021 to place a recall election on the ballot, and close to two thirds of that total have been gathered.

A Message from Lead Proponent Orrin Heatlie:

The RecallGavin2020 team has made it as easy as possible for anyone to participate. It's as simple as one, two, three.

The official petition is available to download and print from the RecallGavin2020.com website. You may print as many copies as you like, then circulate them. People who sign the petition must be registered to vote in California. But, anybody over 18 may circulate the form. Anybody, including you.

The form is user friendly, easy to fill out and available on standard sized paper. The address to mail it in is printed on the bottom of the form. Simply grab some forms and you too can become a clipboard warrior in this fight!

NOTES

Preface

1. **"address my colleagues":** California State Assembly Media Archive, Floor Session, Mar. 16, 2020, https://www.assembly.ca.gov/media/assembly-floor-session-20200316/video
2. **"very different speech":** California State Assembly Media Archive, Floor Session, Dec. 7, 2020, https://www.assembly.ca.gov/media/assembly-floor-session-20201207/video
3. **"When history called":** Duran, Gil. "Coronavirus Failures—and Kamala's Rise—Thwart Gov. Newsom's Presidential Dreams." *Sacramento Bee*, Aug. 20, 2020, www.sacbee.com/opinion/gil-duran/article245108720.html.

Introduction

4. **"centralized the State's powers":** Kevin Kiley. "Trial Documents in Gallagher and Kiley v. Newsom." *Capitol Quagmire*, https://blog.electkevinkiley.com/trial-documents/
5. **"new progressive era":** "California Governor Gavin Newsom COVID-19 Briefing Transcript April 1: Will Not Reopen Schools This Academic Year." *Rev*, May 6, 2020, www.rev.com/blog/transcripts/california-governor-gavin-newsom-covid-19-briefing-transcript-april-1-will-not-reopen-schools-this-academic-year.
6. **"comparing the leader of the Senate"**: Newsom, Gavin. *Twitter*, Nov. 12, 2020, twitter.com/GavinNewsom/status/1326965439608467457.

7. **"nation's strictest lockdown":** Silver, Nate. *Twitter*, https://www.cnn.com/interactive/2020/health/coronavirus-schools-reopening/

8. **"most new COVID cases":** Hwang, Kellie. "Data Shows California's Coronavirus Surge Is Worst in Nation – by a Big Margin." *San Francisco Chronicle,* Dec. 30. 2020, www.sfchronicle.com/bayarea/article/Data-shows-California-s-coronavirus-surge-is-15834616.php.

9. **"nearly the worst unemployment rate":** Guzman, Zack. "California Tops Hawaii as the State with the Worst Unemployment Picture in the US." *Yahoo! Finance*, Dec. 3, 2020, finance.yahoo.com/news/california-tops-hawaii-with-the-worst-state-unemployment-picture-in-the-us-210306049.html.

10. **"world's fifth largest economy":** "California Now Has the World's 5th Largest Economy." *CBS News*, May 4, 2018, www.cbsnews.com/news/california-now-has-the-worlds-5th-largest-economy/.

11. **"nearly the worst income inequality":** "Data Center: US Data." Population Reference Bureau, www.prb.org/usdata/indicator/gini/table?geos=US.

12. **"highest housing prices":** Buhayar, Noah and Christopher Canon, "How California Became America's Housing Market Nightmare." *Bloomberg*, www.bloomberg.com/graphics/2019-california-housing-crisis/.

13. **"among the worst roads":** "Which States Have the Worst Roads—and Which Have the Best?" https://www.motortrend.com/features-collections/worst-roads-in-america-ranked-by-state/?slide=49

14. **"worst education for poor students":** Calefati, Jessica. "California's Poor Students Rank next to Last on National Test." *CalMatters*, June 23, 2020, *CalMatters*.org/education/2018/04/californias-poor-students-rank-next-to-last-on-national-test/.

15. **"A recent survey":** Martichoux, Alix. "53 Percent of Californians Want to Leave the State, According to New Survey." *SFGATE*, *San Francisco Chronicle*, Feb. 14, 2019, www.sfgate.com/expensive-san-francisco/article/move-out-of-bay-area-california-where-to-go-cost-13614119.php.

16. **"Unlivable":** Lowrey, Annie. "California Is Becoming Unlivable." *The Atlantic*, Oct. 31, 2019, www.theatlantic.com/ideas/archive/2019/10/can-california-save-itself/601135/.

17. **"Anyone":** Berman, Richard. "Why Would Anyone Live in California?" *The Washington Times*, Sept. 23, 2019, www.washingtontimes.com/news/2019/sep/23/why-would-anyone-live-in-california/.

18. **"The End":** Manjoo, Farhad. "It's the End of California as We Know It." The *New York Times*, The *New York Times*, Oct. 30 2019, www.nytimes.com/2019/10/30/opinion/sunday/california-fires.html.

19. **"Survive":** Morain, Dan. "How Does California Ever Survive?" *CalMatters*, Nov. 14 2019, *CalMatters*.org/newsletters/whatmatters/2019/11/how-does-california-ever-survive/.

20. **"Premodern":** Hanson, Victor Davis. "Has California Become 'Premodern'?" *Arkansas Online*, Oct. 31 2019, www.nwaonline.com/news/2019/oct/31/victor-davis-hanson-has-california-beco/.

21. **"Deepened poverty and inequality":** Botts, Jackie, et al. "How COVID Is Worsening California's Income Inequality." *CalMatters*, Sept. 16 2020, *CalMatters*.org/economy/2020/07/california-covid-deepening-income-inequality-data/.

22. **"achievement gaps in our schools":** Singh, Maanvi. "How California Went from a Leader in the Covid Fight to a State in Despair." *The Guardian*, Dec. 29, 2020, www.theguardian.com/us-news/2020/dec/28/how-california-went-from-leader-covid-fight-despair.

23. **"PPIC poll":** "Most Think California Children Will Be Worse Off than Their Parents; Two-Thirds See Income Inequality Widening." Public Policy Institute of California, Dec. 11, 2020, www.ppic.org/press-release/most-think-california-children-will-be-worse-off-than-their-parents-two-thirds-see-income-inequality-widening/.

24. **"worst population growth":** Gardiner, Dustin. "'This Isn't the Golden State of the Past': California Is Barely Growing." *San Francisco Chronicle*, Dec. 17 2020, www.sfchronicle.com/politics/article/This-isn-t-the-Golden-State-of-the-past-15809080.php.

25. **"Gavin Newsom's 2022 reelection":** Newsom for California Governor 2022, *Cal-Access*, http://cal-access.sos.ca.gov/Campaign/Committees/Detail.aspx?id=1375287

26. **"the lobbyist being feted":** Fang, Lee. "Hollywood Deployed Lobbyists to Win Exemptions to Strict California Lockdown." *The Intercept*, Dec. 11, 2020, theintercept.com/2020/12/11/hollywood-covid-filming-california-lockdown/.

27. **"Chair of the Appropriations Committee":** Gonzalez for Assembly 2020; Lorena, *Cal-Access*, http://cal-access.sos.ca.gov/Campaign/Committees/Detail.aspx?id=1414350

28. **"higher lawmaking":** Ackerman, Bruce. *We The People: Foundations.* (New York: Belknap Press, 1993), 31

29. **"unlock the special interest grip":** Schecter, David, "California's Right of Removal: Recall Politics in the Modern Ara." California Politics and Policy, Dec. 2008.

30. **"to prematurely declare an end":** Available upon request.

31. **"I publicly proposed conditions":** Assemblyman Kevin Kiley, *Facebook*, June 16, 2002, https://www.facebook.com/watch/live/?v=187637179310392&ref=search

32. **"extraordinary writ":** Kiley, Kevin, "Briefs Filed with the Court of Appeals," *Capitol Quagmire*, "https://blog.electkevinkiley.com/briefs-filed-with-the-california-court-of-appeals/

33. **"including Dr. Anthony Fauci":** McSweeney, Eoin. "Fauci: 'Close the Bars and Keep the Schools Open' in New York City." *CNN*, Nov. 30, 2020, www.cnn.com/world/live-news/coronavirus-pandemic-11-29-20-intl/h_f3ffeaa97e43a34c99625bccd9b5f195.

34. **"Senator Holly Mitchell":** Letter from Holly Mitchell to Keely Martin Bosler, Oct. 7, 2020, https://*CalMatters*.org/wp-content/uploads/2020/10/FINAL-JLBC-to-DOF-Section-11.90-Homekey-10-7-2020.pdf

35. **"Assemblyman Phil Ting":** Beam, Adam. "Governor's Increased

Spending Draws Concern from Lawmakers." *Associated Press*, May 22, 2020, apnews.com/article/4d7c6095fd96840f534914ab6d220d04.

36. **"no way":** Duran, "Coronavirus Failures."

37. **"did not see":** "Gavin Newsom's Hypocritical French Laundry Fiasco Harms California's COVID-19 Efforts." *Sacramento Bee*, www.sacbee.com/opinion/editorials/article247181176.html.

Chapter 1: The Mario Kart Governor

38. **"Mario Kart-style":** Newsom, Gavin. *Twitter*, Dec. 23, 2019, https://twitter.com/GavinNewsom/status/1209132103088013313

39. **"Twitter profile"**: White, Jeremy B. and Carla Marinucci, "TRUMP Unloads on PELOSI, NEWSOM." *Politico*, Jan. 6 2020, www.politico.com/newsletters/california-playbook/2020/01/06/trump-unloads-on-pelosi-newsom-warren-sanders-bloomberg-steyer-make-ca-moves-down-a-house-seat-cadem-settles-over-bauman-487987.

40. **"brief mention":** Ibid.

41. **"an in-depth article":** Luna, Taryn and Phil Willon, "Gavin Newsom's Ambitious and Uneven First Year as California Governor." *Los Angeles Times,* Jan. 5, 2020, www.latimes.com/california/story/2020-01-05/first-year-california-governor-gavin-newsom.

42. **"a top staffer":** White, Jeremy B. et al. "Legislative Frustrations Simmered during Newsom's First Session as Governor." *Politico,* Oct. 7, 2019. www.politico.com/states/california/story/2019/10/07/legislative-frustrations-simmered-during-newsoms-first-session-as-governor-1203896.

43. **"the feeling":** Ibid.

44. **"trust and communication":** Pawel, Miriam. "Does Gavin Newsom Have the Grit to Take On the Coronavirus?" *The New York Times*, Apr. 19. 2020. www.nytimes.com/2020/04/19/opinion/gavin-newsom-california-coronavirus.html.

45. **"Governor's allies":** Luna and Willon

46. **"blunders":** Ibid.

47. **"several examples":** Ibid.

48. **"getting publicity":** White, et al.

49. **"nickname":** "Gov. Gaslight? Newsom's Slippery Words on High-Speed Rail Raise Questions." *Sacramento Bee*, Feb. 15, 2020, www.sacbee.com/opinion/editorials/article226360910.html.

50. **"orchestrated"**: Rosenhall, Laurel. "Gavin Newsom's First Rodeo: In Year One, the Governor Bucks Both Donald Trump and Jerry Brown." *CalMatters*, Oct. 14, 2019, *CalMatters*.org/politics/2019/10/gavin-newsoms-first-year-governor-veto-sign-california-trump/.

51. **"habit of overhyping":** Luna and Willon

52. **"many California political observers":** Cava, Marco della. "A Year in, Gavin Newsom Is Still Fighting Trump. Is He Doing Enough to Govern California?" *USA Today*, Dec. 23, 2019, www.usatoday.com/story/news/nation/2019/12/15/gavin-newsom-recall-donald-trump-california-governor/4412013002/.

53. **"bust":** Ibid.

54. **"foster a national profile":** Rosenhall, Laurel. "Gavin Newsom's First Rodeo: In Year One, the Governor Bucks Both Donald Trump and Jerry Brown." *CalMatters*, Oct. 14, 2019, *CalMatters*.org/politics/2019/10/gavin-newsoms-first-year-governor-veto-sign-california-trump/.

55. **"turned his attention":** Koseff, Alexei. "How Newsom's Campaign Promises Have Fared One Year into Term." *San Francisco Chronicle*, Jan. 5, 2020, www.sfchronicle.com/politics/article/How-Newsom-s-campaign-promises-have-fared-one-14948939.php.

56. **"used his platform":** Rosenhall.

57. **"resistance":** Cava.

58. **"first year:** Ibid.

59. **"Newsom himself":** Ronayne, Kathleen. "California's Gov. Newsom Had 'Baptism by Fire' in 1st Year." *Associated Press*, Dec. 30, 2019, www.wsls.com/news/politics/2019/12/30/californias-gov-newsom-had-baptism-by-fire-in-1st-year/.

60. **"the disconnect":** Cava.

61. **"end of his first year":** Luna and Willon.

62. **"homelessness czar":** Koseff, "How's Newsom's Campaign Promises Have Fared."

63. **"1,039 homeless died":** Goodheart, Jessica. "The Geography of Despair: Homeless Deaths Are L.A.'s Other Epidemic." *Capital & Main,* June 19, 2020, capitalandmain.com/geography-of-despair-homeless-deaths-are-los-angeles-other-epidemics-0617.

64. **"highest concern":** Anderson, Bryan. "Top Priority for California Voters Heading into 2020 Primary? Homelessness." *Sacramento Bee*, Jan. 15, 2020, www.sacbee.com/news/politics-government/capitol-alert/article239325588.html.

65. **"extraordinary step":** Office of Governor Gavin Newsom. "Governor Newsom Delivers State of the State Address on Homelessness," Feb. 20, 2020. www.gov.ca.gov/2020/02/19/governor-newsom-delivers-state-of-the-state-address-on-homelessness/.

66. **"along with the plans":** Elias, Thomas D. "One Year in, Newsom's Left 'Biggest Problem' Unsolved." *Daily News*, Dec. 21, 2019, www.dailynews.com/2019/12/21/one-year-in-newsoms-left-biggest-problem-unsolved/.

67. **"corporate greed":** Grimes, Katy. "Gov. Newsom Blames 'Dog-Eat-Dog Capitalism' as Millions of Californians Are in Darkness." *California Globe*, Oct. 30, 2019, californiaglobe.com/section-2/gov-newsom-blames-dog-eat-dog-capitalism-as-millions-of-californians-are-in-darkness/.

68. **"past two decades":** MacMillan, Douglas and Neena Satija. "PG&E Helped Fund the Careers of Calif. Governor and His Wife. Now He Accuses the Utility of 'Corporate Greed.'" *Washington Post*, Nov. 12, 2019, www.washingtonpost.com/business/2019/11/11/pge-helped-fund-

careers-calif-governor-his-wife-now-he-accuses-utility-corporate-greed/.

69. **"Newsom receiving more":** Ibid.

70. **"Jerry Brown":** Ibid.

71. **"refused":** Assembly Bill No. 2079, *California Legislative Information,* leginfo.legislature.ca.gov/faces/billHistoryClient.xhtml?bill_id=201920200AB2079.

72. **"more authoritarian":** Cava

73. **"proved adept":** Pawel, Miriam. "Does Gavin Newsom Have the Grit."

74. **"more than three dozen":** Luna and Willon

75. **"used executive authority":** Ibid.

76. **"What the hell":** Anderson, Bryan. "California Highway Projects Could Lose Gas Tax Funding as Newsom Shifts Money to Mass Transit." *Sacramento Bee*, Oct. 8, 2019, www.sacbee.com/news/politics-government/capitol-alert/article235925402.html.

77. **"Jerry Brown also opposed":** Walters, Dan. "Commentary: Gavin Newsom Does It Again with Death Row Reprieve." *CalMatters*, Mar. 18, 2019, *CalMatters*.org/commentary/2019/03/gavin-newsom-death-row-reprieve/.

78. **"two years before":** Ibid.

79. **"will of the electorate":** Egelko, Bob, and Alexei Koseff. "Gov. Newsom to Order Halt to California's Death Penalty." *San Francisco Chronicle*, Mar. 13, 2019, www.sfchronicle.com/news/article/Gov-Newsom-orders-halt-to-California-s-death-13683693.php.

80. **"granting a reprieve":** Ibid.

81. **"California hadn't executed":** Ibid.

82. **"well orchestrated":** Walters, "Newsom does it again."

83. **"signed a bill":** Office of Governor Gavin Newsom. "Governor Gavin Newsom Signs SB 27: Tax Transparency Bill," July 30, 2019, www.gov.ca.gov/2019/07/30/governor-gavin-newsom-signs-sb-27-tax-

transparency-bill/.

84. **"reason cited":** Siders, David. "Jerry Brown Vetoes Bill to Pry Loose Trump's Tax Returns." *Politico*, Oct. 16, 2017, www.politico.com/story/2017/10/16/jerry-brown-trump-tax-returns-bill-243799.

85. **"moral duty":** Office of Governor Gavin Newsom, "Governor Gavin Newsom Signs SB 27."

86. **"the voters":** Melley, Brian. "California Court Invalidates Law Requiring Trump Tax Returns." *Associated Press*, Nov. 22, 2019, apnews.com/article/9a3dec6fa5684ebb9760e9a9f02bde48.

87. **"searched the record":** "President Trump Wins Big in California – Thanks to Gov. Newsom's Silly Tax Returns Law." *Sacramento Bee*, Nov. 21, 2019, www.sacbee.com/opinion/article237629564.html.

88. **"scripted":** "Read Gov. Gavin Newsom's Inaugural Address." *Los Angeles Times*, Jan. 7, 2019, www.latimes.com/politics/la-pol-governor-gavin-newsom-inaugural-speech-20190107-htmlstory.html.

89. **"will be progressive":** Ibid.

Chapter 2: California's Cruelest Law

90. **"most destructive":** McCarthy, Kevin and Vince Fong, "Opinion: Why Assembly Bill 5 Will Hurt, Not Help, Freelancers." *Digiday*, Jan. 10, 2020, digiday.com/media/op-ed-ab-5-will-hurt-not-help-freelancers/.

91. **"Willie Brown":** Marinucci, Carla. "Willie Brown Gets Assist from Newsom to Keep Writing Chronicle Column." *Politico,* Sept. 4, 2020, www.politico.com/states/california/story/2020/09/04/former-sf-mayor-willie-brown-ensnared-by-ab5-gets-assist-from-newsom-1315782.

92. **"Andrew Cuomo":** Rubinstein, Dana et al. "California Narrative Casts a Pall over East Coast Efforts to Elevate Gig Economy Workers." *Politico,* Mar. 2, 2020, www.politico.com/states/new-york/city-hall/story/2020/03/02/california-narrative-casts-a-pall-over-east-coast-efforts-to-elevate-gig-economy-workers-1264378.

93. **"liberal Daily Kos":** Kos. "Democrats across the Country Seek to Make California's Mistake, Destroying Careers of Freelancers." *Daily Kos*, Jan. 17, 2020. www.dailykos.com/stories/2020/1/17/1912158/-Democrats-across-the-country-seek-to-make-California-s-mistake-destroying-careers-of-freelancers.

94. **"asinine":** Ibid.

95. **"disastrous," "shameful":** Markos Moulitsas, *Twitter*, Apr. 20, 2020, https://twitter.com/markos/status/1252355159788666885

96. **"The NAACP":** "White-Collar, White Professionals Get AB5 Exemptions. Why Don't Black and Brown App-Based Drivers?" *Observer News*, Sept. 9, 2020, ognsc.com/2020/09/08/white-collar-white-professionals-get-ab5-exemptions-why-dont-black-and-brown-app-based-drivers/.

97. **"Black Chamber":** "Statement by Edwin Lombard, CEO CA Black Chamber of Commerce on the Future of AB5." *Business Wire*, June 9, 2020, www.businesswire.com/news/home/20200609005799/en/Statement-Edwin-Lombard-CEO-CA-Black-. Chamber?fbclid=IwAR3 4tDTQOh29rMEftr8DB5JevMmYDMWMJc9mXBq8ZLjPJm66ysss6_pDPnA#.XuD643iFS1c.facebook

98. **"Ph.D. economists":** Evers, Williamson M. "Open Letter to Suspend California AB-5: From 153 Economists and Political Scientists in California:." *Independent Institute*, Apr. 14, 2020, www.independent.org/news/article.asp?id=13119.

99. **"One commentator":** Jackson, Kerry. "Is There Any Way to Escape Punishment of AB5?" *Pacific Research Institute*, Aug. 27, 2020, www.pacificresearch.org/is-there-any-way-to-escape-punishment-of-ab5/.

100. **"shut down":** Kukura, Joe. "Uber and Lyft Will Not Shut Down at Midnight After Last-Minute Reprieve." *SFist*, Aug. 20, 2020, sfist.com/2020/08/20/uber-and-lyft-get-last-minute-reprieve-will-not-shut-down-at-midnight/.

101. **"a judge issued":** Ibid.

102. **"Proposition 22":** Conger, Kate. "Uber and Lyft Drivers in California Will Remain Contractors." *New York Times*, Nov. 4, 2020, www.nytimes.com/2020/11/04/technology/california-uber-lyft-prop-22.html.

103. **"actually written":** Billingsley, Lloyd. "Legislator Misclassification: The Key to AB 5." *California Globe*, Feb. 28, 2020, californiaglobe.com/section-2/legislator-misclassification-the-key-to-ab-5/.

104. **"political payoff":** Ohanian, Lee. "As COVID-19 Spreads, California Wages War With Gig Businesses That Would Save The Most Vulnerable." *Hoover Institution*, Mar. 24, 2020, www.hoover.org/research/covid-19-spreads-california-wages-war-gig-businesses-would-save-most-vulnerable.

105. **"vast majority":** Curtis, Laura. "The Fight for Flexibility Continues." *Capitol Insider*, Mar. 25, 2019, capitolinsider.calchamber.com/2019/03/the-fight-for-flexibility-continues/.

106. **"compiled a book":** Kiley, Kevin. "AB 5 Stories. *Capitol Quagmire*, https://blog.electkevinkiley.com/ab-5-stories/

107. **"stories":** Ibid; Kiley, Kevin. "Suspend AB 5 During the Shutdown." *Medium*, https://medium.com/@kevinpkiley/californians-plead-with-governor-to-suspend-ab-5-during-covid-19-crisis-f5c1aedbc24a

108. **"mainly comprised":** Faces of AB5, Twitter, Apr. 14, 2020, https://twitter.com/Ab5Of/status/1250097825448218624

109. **"All-AB-5":** "It's All-AB-5, All-The-Time, As The California Legislature Returns." JD Supra, www.jdsupra.com/legalnews/it-s-all-ab-5-all-the-time-as-the-98535/.

110. **"Assembly Bill 1928":** Assembly Bill No. 1928, *California Legislative Information*, https://leginfo.legislature.ca.gov/faces/billNavClient.xhtml?bill_id=201920200AB1928

111. **"a letter":** Newsom, Gavin."Governor's Message." *Governor's Budget Summary 2020*-21, Jan. 10, 2020, http://www.ebudget.ca.gov/2020-21/pdf/BudgetSummary/GovernorsMessage.pdf

112. **"Addressing the crowd":** Assemblyman Kevin Kiley, Facebook, Jan. 29,

2020, https://www.facebook.com/FolsomTV/videos/782323602287248

113. **"worker protection":** "Newsom Signs Bill Rewriting California Employment Law, Limiting Use of Independent Contractors." *Los Angeles Times*, 18 Sept. 2019, www.latimes.com/california/story/2019-09-18/gavin-newsom-signs-ab5-employees0independent-contractors-california.

114. "**opposed":** Curtis.

115. "**exempted entirely":** Assembly Bill No. 5, *California Legislative Information* https://leginfo.legislature.ca.gov/faces/billNavClient.xhtml?bill_id=201920200AB5

116. **"perfect opportunity":** Kiley, Kevin. *Twitter*, Feb. 14, 2020, https://twitter.com/KevinKileyCA/status/1228371672056467457

117. **"define":** Kiley, Kevin. *Twitter*, Feb. 16, 2020, https://twitter.com/KevinKileyCA/status/1229083565566001152

118. **"failure to address":** Kiley, Kevin. *Twitter*, Feb. 19, 2020, https://twitter.com/KevinKileyCA/status/1230222163380076545

119. **"lobby day":** Kiley, Kevin. *Twitter*, Feb. 3, 2020, https://twitter.com/KevinKileyCA/status/1224437208909676544

120. **"repeal vote":** Kiley, Kevin. *Twitter*, Feb. 27, 2020, https://twitter.com/KevinKileyCA/status/1233126345237880832

121. **"tweet him":** Kiley, Kevin. *Twitter*, Apr. 2, 2020, https://twitter.com/KevinKileyCA/status/1245909410498482209

122. **"stunning":** "Gov. Gavin Newsom California COVID-19 Briefing Transcript April 24." Rev, 6 May 2020, www.rev.com/blog/transcripts/gov-gavin-newsom-california-covid-19-briefing-transcript-april-24.

123. "**denialism":** Kiley, Kevin. *Twitter*, June 16, 2020, https://twitter.com/KevinKileyCA/status/1272967447713218560

124. **"political obituary":** Kiley, Kevin. *Twitter*, Apr. 25, 2020, https://twitter.com/KevinKileyCA/status/1254138631742078976

125. **"latest ensnared":** Marinucci, "Willie Brown Gets Assist."

126. **"signed the bill":** Ibid.

127. **"unions controlled":** Ibid.

128. **"best job":** Cava.

Chapter 3: COVID Begins

129. **"de-prioritizing":** Wiley, Hannah. "Before Coronavirus, California Let 1 in 4 of Its Public Health Labs Close." *Sacramento Bee*, Mar. 29, 2020 www.sacbee.com/news/politics-government/capitol-alert/article241501141.html.

130. **"not recommending":** "Planning Continues for Indian Gaming Tradeshow & Convention in San Diego." *Native News Online*, Mar. 10 2020, nativenewsonline.net/currents/planning-continues-for-indian-gaming-tradeshow-convention-in-san-diego-march-24-27.

131. **"Bay Area":** County of San Mateo, Press Release. "Seven Bay Area Jurisdictions Order Residents to Stay Home." March 16, 2020, www.smcgov.org/press-release/march-16-2020-seven-bay-area-jurisdictions-order-residents-stay-home.

132. **"State of the State":** Office of Governor Gavin Newson. "Governor Newsom Delivers State of the State Address on Homelessness." Feb. 20, 2020, www.gov.ca.gov/2020/02/19/governor-newsom-delivers-state-of-the-state-address-on-homelessness/.

133. **"mentioning COVID-19":** Newsom, Gavin. *Twitter*, search: 2/1/20-2/29/20, https://twitter.com/search?q=(from%3AGavinNewsom)%20until%3A2020-02-29%20since%3A2020-02-01&src=typed_query

134. **"absurd price":** Newsom, Gavin. *Twitter*, Mar. 3, 2020, https://twitter.com/GavinNewsom/status/1234930025108930561

135. **"extraordinary prediction":** "Is Newsom Right? Could California See 25.5 Million Coronavirus Cases in Two Months?" *Los Angeles Times*, Mar. 21, 2020, www.latimes.com/california/story/2020-03-20/newsom-california-25-million-coronavirus-cases-two-months.

136. **"lacked the data":** Ibid.

137. "**not using science":** Ibid.

138. **"walked back":** Ibid.

139. **"recessed":** Myers, John. "California Legislature Extends Recess to May 4 over Coronavirus Concerns." *Los Angeles Times*, Apr. 4, 2020, www.latimes.com/california/story/2020-04-03/california-legislature-extends-recess-over-coronavirus.

Chapter 4: Self-Promotional

140. **"breathlessly advertise":** Office of the Governor of California. *Twitter*, Apr. 23, 2020, https://twitter.com/CAgovernor/status/1253362451191459847

141. **"major announcement":** Office of the Governor of California. *Twitter*, Mar. 19, 2020, https://twitter.com/CAgovernor/status/1240807644111065088

142. **"hundreds of thousands":** Ibid.

143. **"several times more":** Sheeler, Andrew. "Thousands Watch Hearing over Newsom Powers + Machete Speaks + Dirty Tricks Campaign?" *Sacramento Bee*, Oct. 22, 2020, www.sacbee.com/news/politics-government/capitol-alert/article246616913.html.

144. **"fixture":** Luna, Taryn. "Criticism Grows over Gov. Gavin Newsom's Management of the Coronavirus Crisis." *Los Angeles Times*, Apr. 29, 2020, www.latimes.com/california/story/2020-04-29/gavin-newsom-coronavirus-response-criticism-nonprofits-legislators.

145. **"national network":** Marinucci and White, "ROSE PARADE Cancelled," *Politico*, July 16, 2020, www.politico.com/newsletters/california-playbook/2020/07/16/rose-parade-cancelled-sf-corruption-probe-widens-newsom-and-davis-lessons-learned-kanye-in-or-out-navarro-slams-fauci-geffen-gives-big-to-project-lincoln-lada-jackie-lacey-vulnerable-489813.

146. **"you said yes":** "Watch Late Night with Seth Meyers Season 7 Episode 94: Gavin Newsom; Retta on Peacock." *Peacock*, www.peacocktv.com/watch-online/tv/late-night-with-seth-meyers/7677126457258993112/seasons/7/episodes/gavin-newsom-retta-episode-94/d8b476cc-abbf-3000-9f1e-d0e7f3788ac5.

147. **"contain his delight":** Ibid.

148. **"friend of a friend."** Ibid.

149. **"feel good":** Ibid.

150. **"Seth Meyers appearance":** Ibid.

151. **"new policy initiatives":** Luna.

152. **"pull back":** Kilkenny, Katie. "Gov. Gavin Newsom Says California Now Reprising Previously Postponed 'Necessary' Surgeries." *Hollywood Reporter*, Apr. 22, 2020, www.hollywoodreporter.com/news/gov-gavin-newsom-says-california-reprising-previously-postponed-necessary-surgeries-1291363.

153. **"mixed message":** Luna, "Criticism grows."

154. **"Newsom unveiled":** Ibid.

155. **"better way":** Ibid.

156. **"The fact is":** Ibid.

157. **"changed course":** Ibid.

158. **"touted:** Ibid.

159. **"initial claims":** Ronayne, Kathleen. "Newsom's Mask Deal Shows Tendency for Big Plans, Few Details." *Associated Press*, Apr. 15, 2020, apnews.com/article/3d6b9c48746f91c00adf134070a80849.

160. **"falsely claimed":** Ibid.

161. "**keeps shifting"** Ibid.

162. **"youthful face":** Pawel, "Does Gavin Newsom Have the Grit"

163. **"first question":** "Gov. Gavin Newsom California COVID-19 Briefing

Transcript April 13." *Rev*, May 6, 2020, www.rev.com/blog/transcripts/gov-gavin-newsom-california-covid-19-briefing-transcript-april-13.

164. **"The problem":** Luna, "Criticism grows."

165. "would be great": White, Jeremy B. et al. "Newsom: California's Enormous Mask Order Won't Disrupt Supply Chain for Others." *Politico*, Apr. 9, 2020, www.politico.com/states/california/story/2020/04/08/newsom-californias-enormous-mask-order-wont-disrupt-supply-chain-for-others-1274110.

166. **"familiar defense":** Luna.

167. **"I recognize":** "Gov. Gavin Newsom California COVID-19 Briefing Transcript April 21." *Rev*, May 6, 2020, www.rev.com/blog/transcripts/gov-gavin-newsom-california-covid-19-briefing-transcript-april-21.

168. **"carried live":** Littleton, Cynthia. "Andrew Cuomo's Daily Press Conferences Became Must-See Daytime TV." *Variety*, Oct. 8, 2020, variety.com/2020/tv/news/new-york-andrew-cuomo-pandemic-briefings-1234796302/.

169. **"Emmy":** Dwyer, Colin. "Andrew Cuomo To Receive International Emmy For 'Masterful' COVID-19 Briefings." *NPR*, Nov. 21, 2020, www.npr.org/sections/coronavirus-live-updates/2020/11/21/937445923/andrew-cuomo-to-receive-international-emmy-for-masterful-covid-19-briefings.

170. **"White Knight":** Burns, Alexander. "Biden and Cuomo: Friends, Allies and Supporting Players No Longer." *New York Times*, Apr. 11, 2020, www.nytimes.com/2020/04/11/us/politics/biden-cuomo-coronavirus.html.

171. **"well-known":** Mehta, Seema and Melanie Mason. "America's Governors': Andrew Cuomo and Gavin Newsom Take the Lead on Coronavirus," *Los Angeles Times*, Mar. 27, 2020, www.latimes.com/politics/story/2020-03-27/cuomo-newsom-democrats-coronavirus.

172. **"20 times":** Pawel, "Does Gavin Newsom Have the Grit"

173. **"emulated":** Ibid.

174. **"moved swiftly":** Ronayne, Kathleen. "Newsom's Mask Deal."

175. **"scathing editorial":** "Gavin Newsom's Half-Baked Announcements Harm Credibility, Raise Troubling Questions." *Sacramento Bee*, Apr. 29, 2020, www.sacbee.com/opinion/editorials/article242353311.html.

176. **"dramatic":** Board, "Elon Musk's Ventilator Fiasco Shows Need for More Oversight of Gavin Newsom's Mask Deal." *Sacramento Bee*, Apr. 14, 2020, www.sacbee.com/opinion/editorials/article241982586.html.

177. **"weakness":** "By Making a Lobbyist His Top Aide, Gov. Gavin Newsom Raises Troubling Ethical Questions." *Sacramento Bee*, Dec. 10, 2020, www.sacbee.com/opinion/editorials/article247744605.html.

178. **"on message":** White, Jeremy B. *Twitter*, July 2, 2020, https://twitter.com/JeremyBWhite/status/1278779032037814272

179. **"implies":** Walters, Dan. *Twitter*, July 2, 2020, https://twitter.com/Dan*CalMatters*/status/1278806600908603392

180. **"specific meaning":** Walters, Dan. *Twitter*, July 2, 2020, https://twitter.com/Dan*CalMatters*/status/1279043419365507072

181. **"speculation":** Skelton, George. "Newsom and Cuomo Have Been Top Leaders in the Coronavirus Crisis. Don't Count on Them to Challenge Biden." *Los Angeles Times*, Apr. 2, 2020, www.latimes.com/california/story/2020-04-02/skelton-gavin-newsom-andrew-cuomo-coronavirus.

182. **"headline":** Wilkinson, Francis. "Gavin Newsom Declares California a 'Nation State.'" *Bloomberg*, Apr. 9, 2020, www.bloomberg.com/opinion/articles/2020-04-09/california-declares-independence-from-trump-s-coronavirus-plans.

183. **"supportive column":** Ibid.

184. **"scale and scope":** Walters, Dan. "*CalMatters* Commentary: Could California Really Go It Alone?" *CalMatters*, May 10, 2020, www.vcstar.com/story/opinion/columnists/2020/05/10/*CalMatters*-commentary-could-california-really-go-alone/3096852001/.

185. **"career peaked":** Duran, "Coronavirus Failures."

186. **"MSNBC's 6 PM hour":** "Newsom: California Has Deal for 200 Million Masks per Month." *MSNBC,* Apr. 8, 2020, www.msnbc.com/rachel-maddow/watch/newsom-california-has-deal-for-200-million-masks-per-month-81763397587.

187. **"#PresidentNewsom":** Sheeler, Andrew. "#PresidentNewsom Trends on Twitter after California's Governor Appears on Rachel Maddow Show." *Sacramento Bee*, Apr. 8, 2020, www.sacbee.com/news/politics-government/capitol-alert/article241860561.html.

188. **"lobbyist in Sacramento":** Rosenhall, Laurel and Dan Morain. "Amid Pandemic, Newsom Faces Scrutiny over $1B Face-Mask Deal." *CalMatters*, Apr. 14, 2020, *CalMatters*.org/health/coronavirus/2020/04/california-coronavirus-face-masks-gavin-newsom-byd/.

189. **"contributed $40,000":** Ibid.

190. **"wired $457 million":** Rosenhall, Laurel. "Exclusive: California Wires Mask Dealer Half a Billion Dollars, Then Claws It Back." *CalMatters*, Sept. 17, 2020, *CalMatters*.org/health/coronavirus/2020/05/california-mask-deal-blue-flame-collapsed-republican-vendor-maryland-porter-gula-thomas/.

191. **"$800 million contract":** Elmahrek, Adam and Melody Gutierrez. "A Politically Connected Firm Gets an $800-Million Mask Contract with California. Then It Falls Apart." *Los Angeles Times*, May 9, 2020, www.latimes.com/california/story/2020-05-09/coronavirus-california-contracts-masks-bear-mountain.

192. **"national headlines":***Sacramento Bee*, "Elon Musk's Ventilator Fiasco."

193. **"spending authority":** Bollag, Sophia. "California 'Vetting' Masks It's Buying in Deal with Company Barred from Some Transit Bids." *Sacramento Bee*, Apr. 13, 2020, www.sacbee.com/news/politics-government/capitol-alert/article241990106.html.

194. **"informed only minutes":** Pawel, "Does Gavin Newsom Have the Grit"

195. **"two months earlier":** "Trump Blacklisted This Chinese Company. Now It's Making Coronavirus Masks for U.S. Hospitals." *Vice*, Apr. 11,

2020, www.vice.com/en/article/qjdqnb/trump-blacklisted-this-chinese-company-now-its-making-coronavirus-masks-for-us-hospitals.

196. **"performance issues":** St. John, Paige. "Stalls, Stops and Breakdowns: Problems Plague Push for Electric Buses." *Los Angeles Times*, May 20, 2018, www.latimes.com/local/lanow/la-me-electric-buses-20180520-story.html.

197. **"banned BYD":** Newhauser.

198. **"What the hell?":** Ibid.

199. **"exposé":** Ibid.

200. **"no history":** Ibid.

201. **"Sacramento lobbyist."** Rosenhall and Morain.

202. **"defamation lawsuit":** Hugo Guzman. "BYD Files Federal Defamation Lawsuit against VICE." *The Fourth Revolution*, Apr. 28, 2020, www.thefourth-revolution.com/news/byd-files-federal-defamation-lawsuit-against-vice/.

203. **"repeatedly asked":** Bollag, Sophia. "Newsom Administration Says It Won't Release Nearly $1B Contract until It's Sure Masks Will Arrive." *Sacramento Bee*, www.sacbee.com/news/politics-government/capitol-alert/article242073726.html.

204. **"big result":** Pawel, "Does Gavin Newsom Have the Grit"

205. **"public records":** "Newsom Administration Refuses to Divulge Nearly $1-Billion Contract for Coronavirus Masks." *Los Angeles Times*, 5 May 2020, www.latimes.com/california/story/2020-05-04/gavin-newsom-will-not-release-california-coronavirus-masks-byd-contract.

206. **"only generalities":** Pawel, "Does Gavin Newsom Have the Grit."

207. **"imperil delivery":** Ibid.

208. **"stonewalled":** "Newsom Hiding Coronavirus Mask Deal, but California Legislature Has Subpoena Power." *Sacramento Bee*, 22 Apr. 2020, www.sacbee.com/opinion/editorials/article242181691.html.

209. **"It was a month":** Bollag, Sophia, et al. "'Urgency and Panic': Inside

Gov. Gavin Newsom's Rush to Buy Coronavirus Gear." *Sacramento Bee*, May 6, 2020, www.sacbee.com/news/politics-government/capitol-alert/article242556951.html.

210. **"Newsom had paid":** "New Cost Details Emerge in California's Secretive Coronavirus Masks Deal with Chinese Company." *Los Angeles Times*, 6 May 2020, www.latimes.com/california/story/2020-05-06/california-coronavirus-mask-price-byd-coronavirus.

211. **"under a dollar":** "New Cost Details Emerge in California's Secretive Coronavirus Masks Deal with Chinese Company." *Los Angeles Times*, 6 May 2020, www.latimes.com/california/story/2020-05-06/california-coronavirus-mask-price-byd-coronavirus.

212. **"live without":** "California Governor Newsom Coronavirus News Conference." *CSPAN*, May 29, 2020, www.c-span.org/video/?472586-1%2Fcalifornia-governor-newsom-coronavirus-news-conference.

213. **"failed":** Bollag, Sophia. "Federal Regulators Contradict California Gov. Newsom, Say BYD Masks Denied Certification." *Sacramento Bee*, May 13, 2020, www.sacbee.com/news/politics-government/capitol-alert/article242707981.html.

214. **"been delayed"**: Ibid.

215. **"not acceptable":** Ibid.

216. **"refund":** Ronayne, Kathleen. "California to Get $247M Refund as Masks Face Delivery Delay." *Associated Press*, May 7, 2020, apnews.com/article/7105ec5d5f02f611146dcf89995770f9.

217. **"collapsed":** Ronayne, Kathleen. "Expensive California Mask Deal Blows Past Another Deadline." *Associated Press*, June 3, 2020, www.nbcbayarea.com/news/california/expensive-california-mask-deal-blows-past-another-deadline/2302677/.

218. **"null and void":** Gutierrez, Melody. "California Grants Another Extension to BYD in Delivering $1-Billion Order of N95 Masks." *Los Angeles Times*, June 5, 2020, www.latimes.com/california/story/2020-06-05/california-gives-extension-order-byd-n95-masks-

coronavirus.

219. **"resurrect":** Ibid.

220. **"Wild West":** Bollag, Sophia. "'This Is the Wild Wild West.' Gavin Newsom Says More Transparency Could Imperil Mask Deal." *Sacramento Bee*, Apr. 18, 2020, www.sacbee.com/news/politics-government/capitol-alert/article242113051.html.

221. **"three months":** "Chinese Manufacturer Receives Approval to Deliver N95 Masks to California." *JD Supra*, June 26, 2020, www.jdsupra.com/legalnews/chinese-manufacturer-receives-approval-78023/.

222. **"I don't care":** CNN Replay. *Facebook*, Apr. 1, 2020, https://www.facebook.com/watch/?v=599552177570303

223. **"touted":** Marinucci, White, et al.

224. **"Kamala Harris":** White, Jeremy B. and Carla Marinucci. "TAX Time?" *Politico*, Aug. 17, 2020, www.politico.com/newsletters/california-playbook/2020/08/17/tax-time-newsom-blasts-postal-sabotage-as-pelosi-calls-house-back-trump-carson-hit-ca-yimbys-ammo-law-nixed-mccarthy-rivals-plotting-490090.

225. **"transition":** Duran, "Coronavirus failures"

Chapter 5: Lawless

226. **"38th Executive Order":** Office of Governor Gavin Newsom. "Governor Newsom Issues Executive Order to Protect Public Health by Mailing Every Registered Voter a Ballot Ahead of the November General Election." May 8, 2020, www.gov.ca.gov/2020/05/08/governor-newsom-issues-executive-order-to-protect-public-health-by-mailing-every-registered-voter-a-ballot-ahead-of-the-november-general-election/.

227. **"statutory authority":** Executive Order N-64020, https://www.gov.ca.gov/wp-content/uploads/2020/05/05.08.2020-EO-N-64-20-text.pdf

228. **"A bill":** Assembly Bill No. 860, *California Legislative Information*,

https://leginfo.legislature.ca.gov/faces/billHistoryClient.xhtml?bill_id=201920200AB860

229. **"first state":** Office of Governor Gavin Newsom. "Governor Newsom Issues Executive Order to Protect Public Health by Mailing Every Registered Voter a Ballot."

230. "California becomes first": White, Jeremy B. "California Becomes First State to Switch November Election to All-Mail Balloting." *Politico*, May 8, 2020, www.politico.com/states/california/story/2020/05/08/california-becomes-first-state-to-make-november-an-all-mail-ballot-election-1283238.

231. **"Joe Biden":** "Joe Biden Praises Gov. Gavin Newsom's Mail-In Voting Order; Trump Campaign Bashes COVID-19 Deterrent – Update." *Yahoo!*, www.yahoo.com/entertainment/california-full-mail-voting-potus-200959235.html.

232. **"makes California":** Beggin, Riley. "California Will Send All Voters Mail-in Ballots for November's Election." *Vox*, May 9, 2020, www.vox.com/policy-and-politics/2020/5/9/21252974/california-voter-mail-covid-19-november-2020-election.

233. **"I said publicly":** Kiley, Kevin. "A Stunning Abuse of Power." *Capitol Quagmire*, https://blog.electkevinkiley.com/a-stunning-abuse-of-power/.

234. **"unilateral":** Office of Governor Gavin Newsom. "Governor Newsom Signs Executive Order on Safe, Secure and Accessible General Election in November." June 3, 2020, www.gov.ca.gov/2020/06/03/governor-newsom-signs-executive-order-on-safe-secure-and-accessible-general-election-in-november/.

235. **"no Caesar":** Kiley, "Briefs Filed with the California Court of Appeals."

236. **"a document":** Kiley, Kevin. "Overview of Governor Gavin Newsom's Executive Action since March 4, 2020," https://blog.electkevinkiley.com/wp-content/uploads/2020/09/COVID-19-Executive-Orders-updated-09042020-1.pdf

237. **"Constitution":** Willon, Phil. "California's Mask Order Tests the Limits of Newsom's Executive Power." *Los Angeles Times*, June 29, 2020, www.

latimes.com/california/story/2020-06-29/california-mask-order-gavin-newsom-powers-coronavirus.

238. **"16 other codes":** Kiley, "Overview of Governor Gavin Newsom's Executive Action."

239. "centralizes the State's power": Kiley, "Trial Documents in Gallagher and Kiley v. Newsom."

240. **"Accumulation":** James Madison, *The Federalist Papers*. No. 47.

241. **"second of three":** "Gov. Gavin Newsom California COVID-19 Briefing Transcript April 21." *Rev*, May 6, 2020, www.rev.com/blog/transcripts/gov-gavin-newsom-california-covid-19-briefing-transcript-april-21.

242. **"appreciate":** Willon, "California's Mask Order."

243. **"harshest criticism":** Murphy, Katy. "California Lawmakers Deliver Their Harshest Criticism of Newsom Yet." *Politico*, May 22, 2020, www.politico.com/states/california/story/2020/05/22/california-lawmakers-deliver-their-harshest-criticism-of-newsom-yet-1285632.

244. **"Bipartisan lawmakers":** Wiley, Hannah, and Sophia Bollag. "Bipartisan California Lawmakers Criticize Newsom's COVID-19 Spending, Warn of 'Overreach'." *Sacramento Bee*, May 22, 2020. www.sacbee.com/news/politics-government/capitol-alert/article242937681.html.

245. **"cut off":** "Gavin Newsom Has Been Great, but It's Time to Cut off His Blank Check." *Los Angeles Times*, May 22, 2020, www.latimes.com/opinion/story/2020-05-21/gavin-newsom-emergency-budget-power-coronavirus-pandemic.

246. **"Capitol distress":** Riggs, Kevin. "Riggs Report: Capitol Distress over Newsom's Emergency Powers." *KCRA*, May 21, 2020, www.kcra.com/article/riggs-report-capitol-distress-over-newsoms-emergency-powers/32627473.

247. **"Lawmakers of both":** Thompson, Don. "Judge Limits California Governor's Emergency Rule-Making." *Associated Press*, 13 June 2020. apnews.com/article/c16d73c9223c310d0b8b5f2f1c18cb01.

248. **"huge overreach of authority":** Beam, Adam, "Governor's Increased Spending Draws Concern from Lawmakers." *Associated Press*, May 22, 2002, "https://apnews.com/article/4d7c6095fd96840f534914ab6d220d04

249. **"What's the point":** Murphy, Katy. "California Lawmakers Deliver Their Harshest Criticism of Newsom Yet." *Politico*, May 22, 2020, www.politico.com/states/california/story/2020/05/22/california-lawmakers-deliver-their-harshest-criticism-of-newsom-yet-1285632.

250. **"repeatedly called":** Mitchell.

251. **"few friends":** Marinucci, White, et al.

252. **"serious concerns":** Harris, Evan. "Newsom's Executive Orders Are Too Much for State Lawmakers." *Pacific Research Institute*, May 26, 2020, www.pacificresearch.org/newsoms-executive-orders-are-too-much-for-state-lawmakers/.

253. **"troubled":** Ibid.

254. **"letter":** Legislative Analyst's Office. "Initial Comments on the Governor's May Revision." May 21, 2020, lao.ca.gov/Publications/Report/4232.

255. **"unilaterally appropriating":** Grimes, Katy. "Gov. Newsom and Legislature Each Want Additional $200M For Homeless in a Tit-for-Tat Over Pet Projects." *California Globe*, Oct. 9, 2020, californiaglobe.com/section-2/gov-newsom-and-legislature-each-want-additional-200m-for-homeless-in-a-tit-for-tat-over-pet-projects/.

256. **"Resolution":** Assembly Concurrent Resolution No. 196, *California Legislative Information*, http://leginfo.legislature.ca.gov/faces/billTextClient.xhtml?bill_id=201920200ACR196#:~:text=ACR%20196%2C%20as%20introduced%2C%20Kiley,a%20result%20of%20that%20proclamation.

257. **"vaccine timeline":** Kiley, Kevin. *Twitter*, May 23, 2020, https://twitter.com/KevinKileyCA/status/1264314625539010561

258. **"editorial":***Los Angeles Times*, "Time To Cut Off."

259. **"prematurely declare":** May 24, 2020 email from Anthony Williams to

Kevin Kiley, James Gallagher and others.

260. **"Restraining Order":** Harris, Evan. "Newsom's Executive Orders Are Too Much for State Lawmakers." *Pacific Research Institute*, May 26, 2020, www.pacificresearch.org/newsoms-executive-orders-are-too-much-for-state-lawmakers/.

261. **"rushed":** Thompson, Don. "Appeals Judge Halts Limit on Newsom's Emergency Powers." *Associated Press*, June 18, 2020, www.kcra.com/article/appeals-judge-halts-limit-on-newsoms-emergency-powers/32898067.

262. **"stop trying":** "Court Right to Nix Gov. Newsom's Executive Order on Voting." *Orange County Register*, June 16, 2020, www.ocregister.com/2020/06/15/court-right-to-nix-gov-newsoms-executive-order-on-voting/.

263. **"set aside":** Kiley, "Trial Documents in Gallagher and Kiley v. Newsom."

264. **"ousted":** Ibid.

265. **"centralizes":** Ibid.

266. **"no evidence":** Ibid.

267. **"police powers":** Ibid.

268. **"habit":** Ibid.

269. **"Executive Order":** Office of Governor Gavin Newsom. "Governor Newsom Announces California Will Phase Out Gasoline-Powered Cars & Drastically Reduce Demand for Fossil Fuel in California's Fight Against Climate Change." Sept. 23, 2020, www.gov.ca.gov/2020/09/23/governor-newsom-announces-california-will-phase-out-gasoline-powered-cars-drastically-reduce-demand-for-fossil-fuel-in-californias-fight-against-climate-change/.

270. **"leading the nation":** Ibid.

271. **"Legislature had considered":** Assembly Bill No. 40, *California Legislative Information*, http://leginfo.legislature.ca.gov/faces/billHistoryClient.xhtml?bill_id=201920200AB40

272. **"clear violation":** Davenport, Coral. "Trump to Revoke California's Authority to Set Stricter Auto Emissions Rules." *New York Times*, Sept. 17, 2019, www.nytimes.com/2019/09/17/climate/trump-california-emissions-waiver.html.

273. **"chaos":** "Trial Documents in Gallagher and Kiley v. Newsom."

274. **"over 200,000 people":** Sheeler, "Thousands watch hearing."

275. **"foundational principles":** "Trial Documents in Gallagher and Kiley v. Newsom."

276. **"in theory."** Ibid.

277. **"her ruling."** Ibid.

278. **"joint statement":** Thompson, "Judge Limits California Governor's Powers."

279. **"statement of its own":** "Judge: Newsom Overstepped Authority with Mail-in Ballots Mandate." *KCRA*, Nov. 14, 2020, www.kcra.com/article/judge-newsom-overstepped-authority-with-mail-in-ballots-mandate/34675185.

280. **"expect this case":** Willon, Phil. *Twitter*, Nov. 17, 2020, https://twitter.com/philwillon/status/1328897082514497540

281. **"an editorial":** "A needed challenge to Newsom's one-man rule." *Daily News*, Dec. 26, 2020, www.dailynews.com/2020/12/24/a-needed-challenge-to-newsoms-one-man-rule/.

282. **"concentration":** Ibid.

Chapter 6: Corrupt

283. **"net worth":** "Thomas Steyer." *Forbes Magazine*, www.forbes.com/profile/thomas-steyer/?sh=7f962cb473f5.

284. **"dropped out":** Tolan, Casey. "$250 Million Later, Tom Steyer Drops out of Presidential Race after Poor Showing in South Carolina." *Mercury News*, Mar. 1, 2020, www.mercurynews.com/2020/02/29/tom-steyer-drop-out-

presidential-race/.

285. **"$250 million":** Ibid.

286. "shouting match": "Tom Steyer: I've Worked Tirelessly for Racial Justice – CNN Video." *CNN*, Feb. 26, 2020, www.cnn.com/videos/politics/2020/02/26/tom-steyer-joe-biden-private-prisons-south-carolina-debate-bts-ac360-vpx.cnn.

287. **"$75 million":** Schwartz, Brian. "Tom Steyer Shuts down His Need to Impeach Operation after Failed 2020 Bid, Trump Acquittal." *CNBC*, Apr. 16, 2020, www.cnbc.com/2020/04/16/2020-election-tom-steyer-shuts-down-need-to-impeach-operation.html.

288. **"largest":** Golden, Vaughn. "Tom Steyer, the Top All-Time Democratic Donor, Enters Presidential Field." *OpenSecrets News*, July 9, 2019, www.opensecrets.org/news/2019/07/tom-steyer-enters-2020presidential-field/.

289. **"independent expenditures":** "Who Are the Biggest Donors?" *OpenSecrets*, www.opensecrets.org/elections-overview/biggest-donors.

290. "**wrote checks":** Steyer, Thomas S. *Cal-Access*, http://cal-access.sos.ca.gov/Campaign/Committees/Detail.aspx?id=1252916&view=contributions&session=2015

291. **"tapped Steyer":** Office of Governor Gavin Newsom, "Governor Newsom Taps California Business, Labor, Health Care and Community Leaders for New Task Force on Business and Jobs Recovery." May 5, 2020, www.gov.ca.gov/2020/04/17/governor-newsom-taps-california-business-labor-health-care-and-community-leaders-for-new-task-force-on-business-and-jobs-recovery/.

292. **"commission was charged":** Ibid.

293. **"We needed":** Kiley, Kevin. *Twitter*, Apr. 17, 2020, https://twitter.com/KevinKileyCA/status/1251236216160182272

294. **"Green New Deal":** Jacobs, Emily. "AOC Isn't Talking about Billionaire Tom Steyer Donating to Her Campaign." *New York Post*, Dec, 27, 2019, nypost.com/2019/12/26/aoc-isnt-talking-about-billionaire-tom-steyer-

donating-to-her-campaign/.

295. **"The torrent":** Washington, Kerry. "The Left-Wing Agenda of Newsom's Re-opening Task Force." *Orange County Register*, Apr. 24, 2020, https://www.ocregister.com/2020/04/24/the-left-wing-agenda-of-newsoms-reopening-task-force/.

296. **"there to reopen":** Ibid.

297. "penchant for ideological confrontation": Walters, Dan. "Newsom's Unwieldy Economic Task Force." *CalMatters*, Apr. 22, 2020, www.record-bee.com/2020/04/23/newsoms-unwieldy-economic-task-force/.

298. **"14 of the 80":** Governor's Task Force on Business and Jobs Recovery, https://www.gov.ca.gov/wp-content/uploads/2020/05/Governors-Task-Force-on-Business-Jobs-Recovery.pdf

299. **"spent twice as much":** California Fair Political Practices Commission. "Big Money Talks," Mar. 2010, https://www.fppc.ca.gov/content/dam/fppc/documents/Education-External-Division/Big_Money_Talks.pdf

300. **"spent millions":** Bollag, Sophia. "Gavin Newsom Raised $50 Million Running for Governor. He Still Has $15 Million Left over." *Sacramento Bee*, Feb. 1, 2019, www.sacbee.com/news/politics-government/capitol-alert/article225389760.html.

301. **"large assortment":** Newsom for California Governor 2018. *Cal-Access*, http://cal-access.sos.ca.gov/Campaign/Committees/Detail.aspx?id=1375287&session=2017

302. **"stay-at-home order":** Office of Governor Gavin Newsom. "Governor Gavin Newsom Issues Stay at Home Order." Mar. 21, 2020, www.gov.ca.gov/2020/03/19/governor-gavin-newsom-issues-stay-at-home-order/.

303. **"keeping needed":** Joseph, Jamie, "AB 5 Keeps Needed Health Care Personnel From Working." *Epoch Times*, Mar. 23, 2020, www.theepochtimes.com/ab-5-keeps-needed-health-care-personnel-from-working_3282494.html.

304. **"wrote a letter":** Kiley, Kevin. *Twitter*, Mar. 12, 2020, https://twitter.com/KevinKileyCA/status/1238238389981212672.

305. **"hundreds more":** Kiley, "Suspend AB 5 During the Lockdown."

306. **"Kirstin":** Ibid.

307. **"financial devastation":** Calzada, Alicia Wagner, "NPPA and ASJA Considering Whether to Appeal after Federal District Court Dismisses Their AB5 Lawsuit and Denies Their Request for an Injunction." *NPPA*, Apr. 22, 2020, nppa.org/news/nppa-and-asja-considering-whether-appeal-after-federal-district-court-dismisses-their-ab5.

308. **"Ph.D. economists":** Independent Institute, "Open Letter to Suspend California AB-5."

309. **"weaponize":** "Where's My PUA? The Ongoing War for Your Worker Classification Status." *The People v. AB5*, Apr. 8, 2020, www.thepeoplevab5.com/blog/wheres-my-pua-the-ongoing-war-for-your-worker-classification-status.

310. **"fines":** "The EDD Trap: Avoiding Trouble for Yourself and Your Clients." *The People v. AB5*, Apr. 3, 2020, www.thepeoplevab5.com/blog/the-edd-trap-avoiding-trouble-for-yourself-and-your-clients.

311. **"I wrote a letter":** Kiley, Kevin, *Twitter*, Mar. 31, https://twitter.com/KevinKileyCA/status/1245121555064999936.

312. **"wrote me back":** Kiley, Kevin, *Twitter*, May. 6, https://twitter.com/KevinKileyCA/status/1258154315996254209.

313. **"$54 billion":** "California Faces a Staggering $54 Billion Budget Deficit Due to Economic Devastation from Coronavirus." *CNBC*, May 7, 2020, www.cnbc.com/2020/05/07/california-faces-a-staggering-54-billion-budget-deficit-due-to-economic-devastation-from-coronavirus.html.

314. **"worst unemployment":** Guzman

315. **"$21 million":** Palomba, Michael. "Governor Newsom's Budget Disregards First Responders and Doubles Down on Wasteful Spending." *San Diego News Desk*, June 11, 2020, www.sandiegonewsdesk.com/2020/06/governor-newsoms-budget-disregards-first-responders-and-doubles-down-on-wasteful-spending/.

316. **"three separate agencies":** Office of Governor Gavin Newsom. "Labor and Workforce Development." May 2020 Revised Budget, http://www.ebudget.ca.gov/2020-21/pdf/Revised/BudgetSummary/LaborandWorkforceDevelopment.pdf.

317. **"spoke directly":** Assemblyman Kevin Kiley. Facebook, May 27, 2020, https://www.facebook.com/watch/?ref=search&v=2487507130162818&external_log_id=336c6d9c-3a2b-4bd4-8e9f-495e65924525&q=Assemblyman%20kiley%20AB%205.

318. **"top political spender":** Fair Political Practices Commission, "Big Money Talks."

319. **"largest affiliate":** UTLA. "Contact Us," www.utla.net/contact-us.

320. **"Janus":***Janus v. AFSCME* (2018) 585 U.S. __, *available at* https://www.supremecourt.gov/opinions/17pdf/16-1466_2b3j.pdf

321. **"make this difficult":** Ring, Edward. "A Catalog of California's Anti-Janus Legislation." *California Policy Center*, https://Californiapolicycenter.org/Wp-Content/Uploads/2017/08/LOGO_v2_white_269x70.Png, 12 June 2018, californiapolicycenter.org/a-catalog-of-californias-anti-janus-legislation/.

322. **"against the CTA":** Johnston, Maureen. "*Friedrichs v. California Teachers Association.*" SCOTUSblog, www.scotusblog.com/case-files/cases/friedrichs-v-california-teachers-association/.

323. **"Research Paper":** UTLA, "The Same Storm, But Different Boats," July 2020, https://www.utla.net/sites/default/files/samestormdiffboats_final.pdf

324. **"tax on billionaires":** Freedberg, Louis. "Schools Shouldn't Open until Safety Is Assured, California Teachers Association Tells State." *Chico Enterprise-Record*, July 9, 2020, www.chicoer.com/2020/07/09/schools-shouldnt-open-until-safety-is-assured-california-teachers-association-tells-state/.

325. **"unique and distinctive":** Wiley, Hannah. "Will California Students Fill Classrooms in the Fall? Newsom Says It Depends on the

District." *Sacramento Bee*, July 14, 2020, www.sacbee.com/news/politics-government/capitol-alert/article244200247.html.

326. **"trailer bill":** Senate Bill No. 98, *California Legislative Information*, https://leginfo.legislature.ca.gov/faces/billTextClient.xhtml?bill_id=201920200SB98

327. **"In my 30 years":** Letter of Opposition, Eric Premack, Charter School Development Center.

328. **"new students":** Hawkins, Mackenzie. "California's New Budget Unfairly Hurts Some of California's Best-Performing Schools, Advocates Say." *Sacramento Bee*, July 3, 2020, www.sacbee.com/news/politics-government/capitol-alert/article243822982.html.

329. **"barred":** Senate Bill No. 98.

330. **"Newsom signed":** Ibid.

331. **"was sued":** Tonsall, Sonseeahray. "Students, Educators Sue California over School Funding Changes in This Year's Budget." *FOX40*, July 29, 2020, fox40.com/news/california-connection/students-educators-sue-california-over-school-funding-changes-in-this-years-budget/.

332. **"I opened":** Fensterwald, John. "California Charter Schools Sue State for Not Funding Additional Students This Year." *EdSource*, July 29, 2020, edsource.org/2020/california-charter-schools-sue-state-for-not-funding-new-students-this-year/637291.

333. **"backtrack":** Senate Bill No. 820, *California Legislative Information*, http://leginfo.legislature.ca.gov/faces/billStatusClient.xhtml?bill_id=201920200SB820

334. **"package of bills":** Office of Governor Gavin Newsom. "Governor Newsom Signs Charter School Legislation 10.3.19," Oct. 3, 2019, www.gov.ca.gov/2019/10/03/governor-newsom-signs-charter-school-legislation-10-3-19/.

335. **"direct attack":** "Open Letter to Gov. Newsom in Support of School Choice." *National Action Network*, May 20 2019, nationalactionnetwork.net/chapter/open-letter-to-gov-newsom-in-support-of-school-choice/.

336. **"resolution":** Izumi, Lance. "SoCal NAACP Chapters Break with Unions Because Charter Schools Work." *Times of San Diego*, May 8, 2019, https://timesofsandiego.com/opinion/2019/05/10/socal-naacp-chapters-break-with-unions-because-charter-schools-work/

337. **"moratorium":** UTLA. "UTLA Demands Halt to Charter Co-Locations and New Charter Approvals," March 27, 2020, www.utla.net/news/utla-demands-halt-charter-co-locations-and-new-charter-approvals.

338. **"same demand":** Sand, Larry. "UTLA Uses the Coronavirus as Excuse to Trash Charters." *Daily News*, Apr. 7, 2020, www.dailynews.com/2020/04/07/utla-uses-the-coronavirus-as-excuse-to-trash-charters/.

339. **"labeled":** Ibid.

340. **"calling on lawmakers":** California Teachers Association. "Legislative Funding Proposal Takes a Pass on Opportunity to Right Decades of Wrongs, Ongoing Racial, Health and Economic Injustice." Press Release, July 28, 2020, www.cta.org/press-release/legislative-funding-proposal-takes-a-pass-on-opportunity-to-right-decades-of-wrongs-ongoing-racial-health-and-economic-injustice.

341. **"surveyed":** Kiley, Kevin. "Survey Results on Newsom's School Closure Order." *Capitol Quagmire*, https://blog.electkevinkiley.com/survey/.

342. **"tried to stop":** Blume, Howard/ "L.A. Teachers Union Opposes Opening Campuses for Students with Disabilities, English Learners." *Los Angeles Times*, Sept. 5, 2020, www.latimes.com/california/story/2020-09-05/l-a-teachers-union-opposes-small-groups-of-students-on-campus.

343. **"private elementary schools":** Cano, Ricardo. "Few California Public Schools Pursuing Elementary Waivers." *CalMatters*, Sept. 24, 2020, *CalMatters*.org/education/2020/09/california-public-schools-elementary-waivers/.

344. **"quickly and intentionally":** City of San Jose." Big City Mayors Urge Leaders To Consider Safely Reopening Schools." Press Release, Oct. 15, 2020, www.sanjoseca.gov/Home/Components/News/News/1981/4699.

345. **"blue ribbon commission":** "'It's Offensive' – Mayor London Breed

Says SFUSD Must Focus On Reopening Classrooms Over Renaming Schools." *CBS San Francisco*, Oct. 15, 2020, sanfrancisco.cbslocal.com/2020/10/16/its-offensive-mayor-london-breed-says-sfusd-must-focus-on-reopening-classrooms-over-renaming-schools/.

346. **"a head start":** Wulff, Rachel. "Sacramento Unified School District, Teachers Unions At Odds Over In-Person Learning." *CBS Sacramento*, Oct. 13, 2020, sacramento.cbslocal.com/2020/10/13/sacramento-natomas-twin-rivers-teachers-distance-learning/.

347. **"I asked":** Assembly Media Archive, Joint Hearing of Assembly Education and Assembly Communication and Conveyance Committees, Oct. 14, 2020, https://www.assembly.ca.gov/media/joint-hearing-communications-conveyance-education-committees-20201014/video

348. **"blasted with text messages":** Gallagher, James. *Twitter*, Dec. 16, 2002, https://twitter.com/J_GallagherAD3/status/1339376869758529536.

349. **"cryptic letter":** California Teachers Association, Letter to Legislative Leaders, Dec. 15, 2020, https://www.politico.com/states/f/?id=00000176-6e57-d30e-a5fe-ffdfe9460000

350. **"Safe Schools for All":** Office of Governor Gavin Newsom. "Governor Newsom Unveils California's Safe Schools for All Plan." Press Release, Dec. 30, 2020, www.gov.ca.gov/2020/12/30/governor-newsom-unveils-californias-safe-schools-for-all-plan/.

351. **"did not open":** Ibid.

352. **"Newsom paid":** *Sacramento Bee*, "By Making a Lobbyist His Top Aide."

353. "**get access":** Koseff, Alexei. "Newsom's French Laundry Dinner Shows How Lobbyists Get Access in Sacramento." *San Francico Chronicle,* Nov. 23, 2020, https://www.sfchronicle.com/politics/article/Newsom-s-French-Laundry-dinner-shows-how-15748441.php

354. **"equivalent":** Ibid

355. **"French Laundry crew":** Ibid.

356. **"deep conversation":** Ibid.

357. **"poster boy":** Koseff, "Newsom's French Laundry Dinner."
358. **"cause the public":** Luna, Taryn and Phil Willon. "Newsom's Friendship with Lobbyist Who Threw French Laundry Party Brings Questions." *Los Angeles Times*, Dec. 31, 2020, www.latimes.com/california/story/2020-12-31/questions-linger-newsom-french-laundry-lobbyist.
359. **"exemption":** Fang.
360. **"Sacramento lobbyist":** Rosenhall and Morain.
361. **"Jim DeBoo":** White, Jeremy B. and Victoria Colliver. "Newsom Hires a Capitol Insider with Experience – and Strong Interest Ties." *Politico*, Dec. 9, 2020, www.politico.com/states/california/story/2020/12/09/newsom-hires-a-capitol-insider-with-experience-and-strong-interest-ties-1344308.
362. **"keys to the castle."** *Sacramento Bee*, "By Making a Lobbyist His Top Aide."
363. **"former lobbyists":** Koseff, "Newsom's French Laundry Dinner."
364. **"Chief Ethics Advisor":** "New Ethics Rules Give Gov. Newsom Some Political Cover." *Orange County Register*, Dec. 19, 2020, www.ocregister.com/2020/12/19/new-ethics-rules-give-gov-newsom-some-political-cover/.
365. **"Steyer announced":** "Tom Steyer, the Top All-Time Democratic Donor, Enters Presidential Field." *OpenSecrets News*, July 9, 2019, www.opensecrets.org/news/2019/07/tom-steyer-enters-2020presidential-field/.
366. **"meaningful":** Walters, Dan. "Newsom's Unwieldy Economic Task Force Unlikely to Save California." *CalMatters*, Apr. 22. 2020, www.sacbee.com/opinion/op-ed/article242178461.html.
367. **"disbanded":** Office of Governor Gavin Newsom. "Governor Releases Task Force on Business and Jobs Recovery Report." Press Release, Nov. 20, 2020, www.gov.ca.gov/2020/11/20/carecoverytaskforcereport/.
368. **"no specific new initiatives":** Marinucci, Carla. "Newsom Ends California Economic Task Force despite Widespread Pandemic Closures." *Politico*, Nov. 20, 2020, www.politico.com/states/california/

story/2020/11/20/newsom-ends-california-economic-task-force-despite-widespread-pandemic-closures-1337448.

369. **"months after":** Willon, Phil. "The All-Star Economic Task Force Advising Newsom during the Pandemic Remains a Mystery." *Los Angeles Times*, Aug. 10, 2020, www.latimes.com/california/story/2020-08-10/newsom-coronavirus-economic-task-force.

370. **"star chamber":** Ibid.

371. **"Steve Maviglio":** Ibid.

372. **"Bob Iger":** Myers, John. "Disney's Bob Iger Resigns from Newsom Task Force as Tensions Mount over Theme Park Closures." *Los Angeles Times*, Oct. 2, 2020, www.latimes.com/california/story/2020-10-01/disney-bob-iger-resigns-gavin-newsom-economic-task-force-theme-park-closures.

Chapter 7: Unscientific

373. **"re-opening":** Newsom, Gavin. *Twitter,* Search: science, https://twitter.com/search?q=science%20(from%3AGavinNewsom)&src=typed_query&f=live

374. **"West Coast":** Ibid.

375. **"led by data":** Ibid.

376. **"isn't about politics"**: Ibid.

377. **"Dr. Fauci":** Ibid.

378. **"Twenty-six":** Ibid.

379. **"unwillingness":** "Heather Mac Donald Quotes." *BrainyQuote*, images.brainyquote.com/quotes/heather_mac_donald_1075682?src=t_scientific_method.

380. **"hard close":** "Gov. Gavin Newsom California COVID-19 Briefing Transcript April 30." *Rev*, May 6, www.rev.com/blog/transcripts/gov-gavin-newsom-california-covid-19-briefing-transcript-april-30.

381. **"disturbing images":** Ibid.

382. **"evidence"**: Ibid.

383. **"Nate Silver":** Silver, Nate. *Twitter,* Apr. 30, 2020, https://twitter.com/NateSilver538/status/1255867916853092354.

384. **"livid":** Taxin, Amy. "California Governor's Beach Closure Order Sparks Anger." *Associated Press*, Apr. 30, 2020, apnews.com/article/2903c0c62f97116e9ef6f5425ad0a7ac.

385. **"Michelle Steel":** Ibid.

386. "**Mayor":** Goffard, Christopher. "Protest with an Orange County Twist." *Los Angeles Times*, May 3, 2020, enewspaper.latimes.com/infinity/article_share.aspx?guid=23e9ee25-ac12-47c7-9e15-d9af5944945f&utm_source=veooz&utm_medium=referral.

387. **"clumsy rollout":** Taxin and Beam.

388. **"a lie":** Marinucci, Carla. "Newsom Considered Statewide Beach Closure despite Publicly Dismissing Idea." *Politico*, May 1, 2020, www.politico.com/states/california/story/2020/04/30/newsom-considered-statewide-beach-closure-despite-publicly-dismissing-idea-1281618#:~:text=Newsom%20considered%20statewide%20beach%20closure%20despite%20publicly%20dismissing%20idea,-By%20CARLA%20MARINUCCI&text=OAKLAND%20%E2%80%94%20Gov.&text=Newsom%20on%20Thursday%20instead%20announced,beaches%20only%20in%20Orange%20County.

389. **"not closing":** Mazzei, Patricia, et al. "Frustrated by Crowds, Coastal States Weigh What to Do About Beaches." *New York Times*, Apr. 30, 2020, www.nytimes.com/2020/04/30/us/newsom-beaches-california-coronavirus.html.

390. **"strictest regulations":** Silver, Nate. *Twitter,* Dec. 1, 2020, https://twitter.com/NateSilver538/status/1333924752126308356.

391. **"bowling":** McDuff, Tammye. "Bowling Centers in Distress: Newsom Keeps Bowlers Off the Lanes." *Cerritos Community News*, Oct. 30, 2020, www.loscerritosnews.net/2020/10/30/bowling-centers-in-distress-

newsom-keeps-bowlers-off-the-lanes/.

392. **"youth sports":** Ream, Evan. "Long-Term Sports Clarity Can Help Our Kids Deal with Virus." *Davis Enterprise*, Nov. 1. 2020, www.davisenterprise.com/sports/long-term-sports-clarity-can-help-our-kids-deal-with-virus/.

393. **"curfews":** "See Coronavirus Restrictions and Mask Mandates for All 50 States." *New York Times*, Apr. 25, 2020, www.nytimes.com/interactive/2020/us/states-reopen-map-coronavirus.html.

394. **"school closure":** "Map: Where Schools Are Reopening in the US." *CNN*, www.cnn.com/interactive/2020/health/coronavirus-schools-reopening/.

395. **"outdoor dining":** "See Coronavirus Restrictions." *New York Times*

396. **"playgrounds":** "Governor Newsom Reverses Decision to Ban Playgrounds after Fierce Backlash." *KUSI,* Dec. 9, 2020, www.kusi.com/governor-newsom-reverses-decision-to-ban-playgrounds-after-fierce-backlash/.

397. **"most restrictive":** Colliver, Victoria. "Locked-down California Runs out of Reasons for Surprising Surge." *Politico*, Dec. 25, 2020, www.politico.com/news/2020/12/23/california-covid-surge-450315.

398. **"unemployment":** "California Tops Hawaii," *Yahoo! Finance.*

399. **"25 percent":** Department of Labor. "News Release: Revision to Seasonal Adjustment Factors," Aug. 27, 2020, https://www.dol.gov/sites/dolgov/files/OPA/newsreleases/ui-claims/20201637.pdf

400. "**Garth Gilmour":** Ting, Eric. "'They're Ripping Us Apart': Bay Area Small Business Owners Talk New Lockdown." *New Haven Register*, Dec. 7, 2020, www.nhregister.com/bayarea/article/Bay-Area-stay-at-home-lockdown-small-business-new-15778317.php.

401. **"COVID-19 hotspot":** Hwang, Kellie. "Data Shows California's Coronavirus Surge Is Worst in Nation—by a Big Margin." *San Francisco Chronicle*, Dec. 30, 2020, www.sfchronicle.com/bayarea/article/Data-shows-California-s-coronavirus-surge-is-15834616.php.

402. **"if not":** DeRuy, Emily. "Coronavirus: Without California Surge, US Numbers Would Be Declining." *Mercury News*, Dec. 26 2020, www.mercurynews.com/2020/12/24/coronavirus-without-california-surge-us-case-rate-would-be-declining/.

403. **"stunning":** Colliver, Victoria. "Locked-down California Runs out of Reasons for Surprising Surge." *Politico*, 25 Dec. 2020, www.politico.com/news/2020/12/23/california-covid-surge-450315.

404. **"Nate Silver":** Silver, Nate. *Twitter,* Dec. 3, 2020, https://twitter.com/NateSilver538/status/1334558695720673284.

405. **"Business Roundtable":** Luca. Giacomo. "Sacramento Business Groups Urge California to Modify COVID-19 Restrictions." *abc10*, Nov. 11, 2020, www.abc10.com/article/news/health/coronavirus/sacramento-business-groups-urge-california-to-modify-covid-19-restrictions/103-1481f008-4f22-4ce6-aceb-c0ce1e14ba01.

406. **"struck down":** Britschgi, Christian. "California Judge Says Los Angeles County's Outdoor Dining Ban Isn't 'Grounded in Science, Evidence, or Logic'." *Reason*, Dec. 10, 2020, reason.com/2020/12/10/california-judge-rules-that-los-angeles-outdoor-dining-ban-isnt-grounded-in-science-evidence-or-logic/.

407. **"applied it statewide":** Office of Governor Gavin Newsom. "California Health Officials Announce a Regional Stay at Home Order Triggered by ICU Capacity." Press Release, Dec. 4, 2020, www.gov.ca.gov/2020/12/03/california-health-officials-announce-a-regional-stay-at-home-order-triggered-by-icu-capacity/.

408. **"San Diego Court":***Midway Venture LLC vs. County of San Diego*, Case No. 37-2020-000381940-CR-CR-CTL, https://ca-times.brightspotcdn.com/50/ae/dc4b8877464abad243b0efee155d/minute-order-12.16.20%20-%20Midway%20Venture%20LLC%20vs%20County%20of%20SD.pdf.

409. **"restaurant owner":** Powell, Amy. "Restaurant owner shares her frustration over dining ban after film crew sets up craft services next door." *abcnews*, Dec. 5, 2020, https://abc7news.com/los-angeles-country-restaurant-owner-viral-video-coronavirus-restrictions-covid-rates-

cases/8530341/

410. **"confidently implored":** "Gavin Newsom – Handling the Coronavirus in California." The Daily Social Distancing Show, YouTube, Mar. 30, 2020, www.youtube.com/watch?v=trgb5TftaRE+411.%E2%80%9CJulia+Marcus%E2%80%9D%3A+https%3A%2F%2Fwww.newsbreak.com%2Fcalifornia%2Flos-angeles%2Fliving%2F2120060345020%2Fmany-arent-buying-public-officials-stay-at-home-message-experts-say-theres-a-better-way.

411. **"Emily Oster":** Karlamangla, Soumya. "Many Aren't Buying Public Officials' 'Stay-at-Home' Message. Experts Say There's a Better Way." *Los Angeles Times*, Dec. 7. 2020, https://www.latimes.com/california/story/2020-12-07/coronavirus-stay-home-messaging-la-harm-reduction.

412. **"Monica Gandhi":** Ting, Eric. "As COVID-19 Explodes, Was California Too Strict for Its Own Good?" *SFGATE*, Dec. 22, 2020, www.sfgate.com/bayarea/article/California-COVID-lockdown-cases-deaths-businesses-15819841.php.

413. **"curfew":** Martichoux, Alix. "Gov. Newsom Orders Curfew for Most California Counties." *ABC7 Los Angeles*, Nov. 20, 2020, abc7.com/governor-newsom-california-curfew-gavin-los-angeles/8101518/.

414. **"Mark Cullen":** Vainshtein, Annie. "'The Virus Doesn't Care – Day or Night': Is There Real Science behind COVID Curfews?" *San Francisco Chronicle*, Nov. 20, 2020, www.sfchronicle.com/bayarea/article/Newsom-is-weighing-a-California-curfew-to-help-15740669.php#:~:text=%E2%80%9CThe%20virus%20doesn't%20care,of%20itself%20address%20the%20problem.%E2%80%9D.

415. **"Lee Riley":** Pena, Luz. "Bay Area Businesses Adjust to New California COVID-19 Related Curfew, Some Police Departments Won't Enforce It." *ABC7 San Francisco*, Nov. 22, 2020, abc7news.com/coronavirus-curfew-covid-oakland-sf/8157992/.

416. **"six indicators":** Office of Governor Gavin Newsom. "Governor Newsom Outlines Six Critical Indicators the State Will Consider Before Modifying the Stay-at-Home Order and Other COVID-19 Interventions."

Press Release, Apr. 14, 2020, www.gov.ca.gov/2020/04/14/governor-newsom-outlines-six-critical-indicators-the-state-will-consider-before-modifying-the-stay-at-home-order-and-other-covid-19-interventions/.

417. **"Resilience Roadmap":** West., Beth. "Governor Newsom Announces the Gradual Beginning of Stage 2 of California's Re-Opening Plan." *The Law and Employment Law Blog,* May 8, 2020, https://www.thelelawblog.com/2020/05/articles/new-legislation-and-regulations/governor-newsom-announces-the-gradual-beginning-of-phase-2-of-californias-re-opening-plan/.

418. **"attestation opportunity":** California Department of Public Health Announces New Regional Variance Opportunity, www.cdph.ca.gov/Programs/OPA/Pages/NR20-091.aspx.

419. **"whole categories":** Myers, John et al. "Newsom Orders Bars Closed in 7 California Counties, Including L.A., Due to Coronavirus Spread." *Los Angeles Times,* June 28, 2020, www.latimes.com/california/story/2020-06-28/gavin-newsom-orders-bars-closed-in-7-california-counties-due-to-coronavirus-spread.

420. "**Blueprint":** Office of Governor Gavin Newsom. "Governor Newsom Unveils Blueprint for a Safer Economy, a Statewide, Stringent and Slow Plan for Living with COVID-19." Press Release, Aug. 28, 2020, https://www.gov.ca.gov/2020/08/28/governor-newsom-unveils-blueprint-for-a-safer-economy-a-statewide-stringent-and-slow-plan-for-living-with-covid-19/#:~:text=sub%20menu%20toggle-,Governor%20Newsom%20Unveils%20Blueprint%20for%20a%20Safer%20Economy%2C%20a%20Statewide,for%20Living%20with%20COVID%2D19&text=SACRAMENTO%20%E2%80%93%20Governor%20Gavin%20Newsom%20today,19%20for%20the%20long%20haul.

421. **"Emergency brake":** Office of Governor Gavin Newsom. "Governor Newsom Announces New Immediate Actions to Curb COVID-19 Transmission." Pres Release, Nov. 16, 2020, www.gov.ca.gov/2020/11/16/governor-newsom-announces-new-immediate-actions-to-curb-covid-19-transmission/.

422. **"lab at Stanford":** Ting, "As COVID-19 Explodes."

423. **"Go to a beach":** Newsom, Gavin. *Twitter*, Dec. 10, 2020, https://twitter.com/GavinNewsom/status/1337114326700683265.

424. **"ordered closed":** Kohli, Sonali and Howard Blume. "Public Schools Expected to Remain Closed for the Rest of the Academic Year, Newsom Says." *Los Angeles Times*, Apr. 1, 2020, www.latimes.com/california/story/2020-04-01/coronavirus-school-closures-california.

425. **"released a statement":** Kiley, Kevin. *Twitter*, July 17, 2020, https://twitter.com/KevinKileyCA/status/1284209709067595776.

426. **"overall burden":** Lara S. Shekerdemian, MD. "Outcomes of Children With COVID-19 Admitted to US and Canadian Pediatric Intensive Care Units." *JAMA Pediatrics*, Sept 1, 2020, jamanetwork.com/journals/jamapediatrics/fullarticle/2766037.

427. **"Academy of Pediatrics":** Korioth, Trisha. "AAP Interim Guidance on School Re-Entry Focuses on Mitigating COVID-19 Risks." *American Academy of Pediatrics*, Jan. 5 2021, www.aappublications.org/news/2020/06/26/schoolreopening062620.

428. **"prioritize reopening schools":** National Academies of Science, Engineering, and Medicine. "Schools Should Prioritize Reopening in Fall 2020, Especially for Grades K-5, While Weighing Risks and Benefits." Press Release. July 15, 2020, https://www.nationalacademies.org/news/2020/07/schools-should-prioritize-reopening-in-fall-2020-especially-for-grades-k-5-while-weighing-risks-and-benefits.

429. **"importance of reopening":** Goodnough, Abby. "C.D.C. Calls on Schools to Reopen, Downplaying Health Risks." *New York Times*, July 24, 2020, www.nytimes.com/2020/07/24/health/cdc-schools-coronavirus.html.

430. ***"New York Times":*** "Reopening Schools Will Be a Huge Undertaking. It Must Be Done." *New York Times*, July 11, 2020, www.nytimes.com/2020/07/10/opinion/coronavirus-schools-reopening.html.

431. **"Brookings":** Soland, Jim, et al. "The Impact of COVID-19 on

Student Achievement and What It May Mean for Educators." Brookings, Brookings, May 27, 2020, www.brookings.edu/blog/brown-center-chalkboard/2020/05/27/the-impact-of-covid-19-on-student-achievement-and-what-it-may-mean-for-educators/.

432. **"McKinsey":** Dorn, Emma, et al. "COVID-19 and Student Learning in the United States: The Hurt Could Last a Lifetime." McKinsey & Company, Dec. 14,, 2020, www.mckinsey.com/industries/public-and-social-sector/our-insights/covid-19-and-student-learning-in-the-united-states-the-hurt-could-last-a-lifetime#.

433. **"never logged in":** Richards, Erin. "Students Are Falling behind in Online School. Where's the COVID-19 'Disaster Plan' to Catch Them Up?" *USA Today*, Dec. 17, 2020, www.usatoday.com/in-depth/news/education/2020/12/13/covid-online-school-tutoring-plan/6334907002/.

434. **"Richard Rothstein":** Strauss, Valerie. "Why Covid-19 Will 'Explode' Existing Academic Achievement Gaps." *Washington Post*, Apr. 17, 2020, www.washingtonpost.com/education/2020/04/17/why-covid-19-will-explode-existing-academic-achievement-gaps/.

435. **"Dan Walters":** Walters, Dan. "School Closures May Be Killing Our Kids." *CalMatters*, Dec. 4, 2020, www.theunion.com/opinion/columns/dan-walters-school-closures-may-be-killing-our-kids/.

436. **"American Academy":** Kamenetz, Anya. "U.S. Pediatricians Call For In-Person School This Fall." *NPR*, June 29, 2020, www.npr.org/sections/coronavirus-live-updates/2020/06/29/884638999/u-s-pediatricians-call-for-in-person-school-this-fall%20435.%E2%80%9CEmergency%20Room%20visits%E2%80%9D%3A%20https%3A//losangeles.cbslocal.com/2020/11/16/cdc-mental-health-er-visits-increase-coronavirus//.

437. **"5.5 million":** Christakishttps, Dimitri A. et al. "Estimation of US Children's Educational Attainment and Years of Life Lost Associated With Primary School Closures During the Coronavirus Disease 2019 Pandemic." *Journal of the American Medical Association*, Nov. 12, 2020, https://jamanetwork.com/journals/jamanetworkopen/fullarticle/2772834.

438. **"killing our kids."** Walters, "School Closures"

439. **"Newsom argued":** Wiley, Hannah. "Gov. Newsom Orders Most California Schools to Stay Closed until Coronavirus Spread Lessens." *Sacramento Bee*, July 17, 2020, www.sacbee.com/news/politics-government/capitol-alert/article244301752.html.

440. **"not seen a connection":** Taxin, Amy and Adam Beam. "California sees no link from school openings to virus spread." *Associated Press,* Oct. 6, 2020. https://apnews.com/article/virus-outbreak-public-health-california-eb1dfed46abb53876e07538d5422e40e

441. **"Imperial College":** Wang, Xutong, et al. "Impact of Social Distancing Measures on COVID-19 Healthcare Demand in Central Texas." *MedRxiv*, Jan. 1, 2020, www.medrxiv.org/content/10.1101/2020.04.16.20068403v1.

442. **"little effect":** Zanewi, Du and Michaela Petty. "Impact of Social Distancing Measures on COVID-19 Healthcare Demand in Central Texas," file:///Users/kileyke/Downloads/2020.04.16.20068403v1.full.pdf.

443. **"Finland and Sweden":** Lewis, Nicholas, et al. "COVID-19: Evidence Shows That Transmission by Schoolchildren Is Low," Sept. 22, 2020, www.nicholaslewis.org/covid-19-evidence-shows-that-transmission-by-schoolchildren-is-low/.

444. **"New England Journal":** Geraghty, Jim. "Icelandic Study: 'We Have Not Found a Single Instance of a Child Infecting Parents.'" *National Review*, May 11, 2020, www.nationalreview.com/corner/icelandic-study-we-have-not-found-a-single-instance-of-a-child-infecting-parents/.

445. **"Mark Woolhouse":** Mark McLaughlin, Marc Horne. "School Closures 'a Mistake' as No Teachers Infected in Classroom." *The Times*, Juy 21, 2020, www.thetimes.co.uk/article/school-closures-a-mistake-as-no-teachers-infected-in-classroom-gpppq8r7k.

446. **"Anthony Fauci":** McSweeney, Eoin. "Fauci: 'Close the Bars and Keep the Schools Open' in New York City." *CNN*, Nov. 30, 2020, www.cnn.com/world/live-news/coronavirus-pandemic-11-29-20-intl/h_f3ffeaa97e43a34c99625bccd9b5f195.

447. **"Andrew Cuomo":** Governor Andrew M. Cuomo. "Governor Cuomo Announces That, Based on Each Region's Infection Rate, Schools Across New York State Are Permitted to Open This Fall." Press Release, Aug. 11, 2020, www.governor.ny.gov/news/governor-cuomo-announces-based-each-regions-infection-rate-schools-across-new-york-state-are.

448. **"Massachusetts":** Parnass, Larry. "The Checkup: One New Death, 9 New Cases in Berkshire County." *The Berkshire Eagle*, Oct. 27, 2020, www.berkshireeagle.com/news/local/the-checkup-one-new-death-9-new-cases-in-berkshire-county/article_e1015026-18a1-11eb-a128-1f6e4bf927a0.html.

449. **"startling announcement":** California Health Equity Metric, www.cdph.ca.gov/Programs/CID/DCDC/Pages/COVID-19/CaliforniaHealthEquityMetric.aspx.

450. **"highest poverty":** Walters, Dan. "Commentary: California Still No. 1 in Poverty." *CalMatters*, Sept. 17, 2019, *CalMatters*.org/commentary/2019/09/high-cost-california-no-1-in-poverty/.

451. **"income inequality":** "Data Center: US Data." Population Reference Bureau, www.prb.org/usdata/indicator/gini/table/?geos=US.

452. **"achievement gaps":** Singh, Maanvi. "How California Went from a Leader in the Covid Fight to a State in Despair." *The Guardian*, De. 29, 2020, www.theguardian.com/us-news/2020/dec/28/how-california-went-from-leader-covid-fight-despair.

453. **"locked down":** "Blueprint for a Safer Economy: Equity Focus."

454. **"other states":** Virginia Governor Ralph S. Northam. "Governor Northam Announces Health Equity Pilot Program with City of Richmond." Press Release, May 11, 2020, www.governor.virginia.gov/newsroom/all-releases/2020/may/headline-856730-en.html.

455. **"to some extent":** "Blueprint for a Safer Economy."

456. **"Walter Olsen":** Olsen, Walter. "Before Reopening, California Counties Must Meet 'Equity' Standard." *Cato Institute*, Oct. 7, 2020, www.cato.org/blog/reopening-california-counties-must-meet-equity-standard.

457. **"no green light":** "California Governor Gavin Newsom August 28 Press

Conference Transcript." *Rev*, www.rev.com/blog/transcripts/california-governor-gavin-newsom-august-28-press-conference-transcript.

458. **"separate approval":** Office of Governor Gavin Newsom. "Governor Newsom Names Scientific Safety Review Workgroup to Advise State on COVID-19 Vaccines." Press Release, Nov 6, 2020, www.gov.ca.gov/2020/10/19/governor-newsom-names-scientific-safety-review-workgroup-to-advise-state-on-covid-19-vaccines/.

459. **"Lamar Alexander":** U.S. Senate Committee on Health, Education, Labor & Pensions. "Alexander: New York and California Governors Should Stop Second Guessing FDA on Safety and Efficacy of COVID-19 Vaccines." Press Release, Oct. 24, 2020. www.help.senate.gov/chair/newsroom/press/alexander-new-york-and-california-governors-should-stop-second-guessing-fda-on-safety-and-efficacy-of-covid-19-vaccines.

Chapter 8: Incompetent

460. **"disappeared":** Tapp, Tom. "California Coronavirus Update: Governor Gavin Newsom Silent On State Data Glitch As COVID Deaths Hit Record High." Deadline, Aug. 5, 2020, deadline.com/2020/08/califronia-coronavirus-governor-newsom-quiet-record-death-count-1203005150/.

461. **"apologized":** Taxin, Amy. "Official: California Fixed Glitch That Backlogged COVID Data." *Associated Press*, Aug. 8, 2020, apnews.com/article/san-francisco-virus-outbreak-california-8394ecef9fa842b6d89924c8acb21785.

462. **"resigned."** Myers, John. "California's Public Health Director Resigns in Wake of Coronavirus Data Errors." *Los Angeles Times*, Aug. 10, 2020, www.latimes.com/california/story/2020-08-09/california-public-health-director-resigns-in-wake-of-questions-about-coronavirus-test-data.

463. **"fraud":** Hubler, Shawn. "Unemployment Scam Using Inmates' Names Costs California Hundreds of Millions." *New York Times*, Nov. 24, 2020, www.nytimes.com/2020/11/24/us/california-unemployment-fraud-inmates.html.

464. **"Ellen DeGeneres":** The Ellen DeGeneres Show. "California Gov. Gavin Newsom on What the 'New Normal' Could Look Like." YouTube, Apr. 17, 2020, www.youtube.com/watch?v=OJ676T79q3c+462.%E2%80%9C

465. **"scathing letter":** Letter from California Legislators to Governor Gavin Newsom, Aug. 5, 2020, https://www.voiceofsandiego.org/wp-content/uploads/2020/08/Legislative-EDD-Letter-to-Governor-Newsom.pdf.

466. **"fifth month":** Ibid.

467. **"focus":** Ibid.

468. **"overdue report":** "Gov. Newsom Buried EDD 'Strike Team' Report. Can He Fix California's Unemployment Mess?" *Sacramento Bee*, Sept. 21, 2020, www.sacbee.com/opinion/editorials/article245884720.html.

469. **"growing again":** "CBS13 Investigates EDD Backlog." *CBS Sacramento*, Dec. 28, 2020, https://sacramento.cbslocal.com/video/5148900-cbs13-investigates-edd-backlog/

470. **"1.4 million":** Avalos, George. "Unemployment Fraud: EDD Suspends 1.4 Million Jobless Payments." *Mercury News*, Jan. 8, 2021, www.mercurynews.com/2021/01/07/unemployment-fraud-edd-halt-1-4-million-jobless-payment-covid-economy/.

471. **"#EDDFailoftheDay":** Chiu, David. *Twitter.* June 23, 2020, https://twitter.com/DavidChiu/status/1275456977099882499.

472. **"perfect storm":** McGreevey, Patrick and Kim Christensen. "Californians Battling Unemployment amid Coronavirus Are Stymied by State Agency's Tech Issues." *Los Angeles Times*, Apr. 27, 2020, www.latimes.com/california/story/2020-04-27/coronavirus-california-unemployment-insurance-claims-technology-issues-edd.

473. **"aging and inflexible":** Legislative Analyst's Office. "Unemployment Insurance For Workers Impacted By COVID-19," Mar. 23, 2020, lao.ca.gov/Publications/Report/4208.

474. **"modernization":** Venteicher, Wes, and David Lightman. "Nonstop Calls and No Answers: Why California Wasn't Prepared for Surge in Unemployment." *Sacramento Bee*, Apr. 27. 2020, www.sacbee.com/news/

politics-government/the-state-worker/article242265556.html.

475. **“Other states”:** Pressgrove, Jed. “States Lean on Cloud as Unemployment Claims Skyrocket.” *Government Technology*, Apr. 24, 2020, www.govtech.com/computing/States-Lean-on-Cloud-as-Unemployment-Claims-Skyrocket.html.

476. **“food banks”:** Cohen, Sharon. “Millions of Hungry Americans Turn to Food Banks for 1st Time.” *Associated Press*, Dec. 7, 2020, apnews.com/article/race-and-ethnicity-hunger-coronavirus-pandemic-4c7f1705c6d8ef5bac241e6cc8e331bb.

477. **“press releases”:** Employment Development Department, News Release, “California Workers Struggling Through Pandemic Receive $41.3 Billion in Unemployment Benefits,” July 9, 2020, https://www.edd.ca.gov/About_EDD/pdf/news-20-32.pdf.

478. **“mixed income”:** Christensen, Kim. “Gig Workers Are Now Eligible for Special Unemployment Benefits. But Many Won’t Get Them.” *Los Angeles Times*, May 2, 2020, www.latimes.com/california/story/2020-05-02/coronavirus-unemployment-gig-workers-benefits-pandemic.

479. **“asked”:** Kiley, Kevin. *Twitter,* May 7, 2020, https://twitter.com/KevinKileyCA/status/1258532008923262976.

480. **“wrote a letter”:** Kiley, Kevin. *Twitter,* Apr. 28, 2020, https://twitter.com/KevinKileyCA/status/1255276294666928130.

481. **“agreed”:** Kiley, Kevin. *Twitter,* May 21, 2020, https://twitter.com/KevinKileyCA/status/1263559672553803776.

482. **“Adam Schiff”:** U.S. Congressman Adam Schiff. “Schiff Presses California Labor Agency to Open Application for Pandemic Unemployment Assistance Program.” Press Release, Apr. 10, 2020, schiff.house.gov/news/press-releases/schiff-presses-california-labor-agency-to-open-application-for-pandemic-unemployment-assistance-program.

483. **“fraud”:** Hubler, “Unemployment Scam.”

484. **“35,000”:** Ibid.

485. **"345,000":** "California Jobless Fraud Likely Tops $2 Billion, Bank of America Says." *Associated Press*, Dec. 10, 2020, www.marketwatch.com/story/california-jobless-fraud-likely-tops-2-billion-bank-of-america-says-01607619624.

486. **"$1 billion":** McGreevy, Patrick et al. "California May Have Sent $1 Billion in Jobless Benefits to People Outside the State, D.A.s Warn." *Los Angeles Times*, Dec. 4, 2020, www.latimes.com/california/story/2020-12-04/california-unemployment-benefits-out-of-state-district-attorney.

487. **"$8.5 billion":** Hoeven, Emily. "The Coronavirus Vaccine Arrives in California." *CalMatters*, Dec. 14, 2020, *CalMatters*.org/newsletters/whatmatters/2020/12/coronavirus-vaccine-arrives-california/.

488. **"practical reality":** Gonzalez, Vicki. "EDD Fraud Involving California Inmates: 6 Things to Know about the Massive Scam." *KCRA*, Nov. 25, 2020, www.kcra.com/article/6-things-to-know-about-edd-fraud-involving-california-inmates/34779405.

489. **"names used":** Lyle, Josh. "Scott Peterson Named among Inmates given Money in EDD Unemployment Fraud in California Prisons, Jails." *abc10.Com*, Nov. 24, 2020, www.abc10.com/article/money/edd-fraud-jails/103-b27ee8f8-a0b1-4db3-8645-67316dedad35.

490. **"claimants":** "Media, 13 Stars, and Colonymagazine," Dec. 3, 2020, Issuu, issuu.com/colonymagazine/docs/the_paso_robles_press___dec_3_2020.

491. **"Tens of thousands":** Beam, Adam./ "California Jobless Fraud Likely Tops $2 Billion, Bank Says." *Associated Press*, Dec. 9, 2020, www.kpbs.org/news/2020/dec/08/california-jobless-fraud-likely-tops-2-billion/.

492. **"Hundreds of cards":** Ibid.

493. **"directly to prisons":** Gotfredson, David. "EDD Suspends Some Claims Pending Identity Verification." *CBS8*, Jan. 5, 2021, www.cbs8.com/article/money/edd-suspends-some-claims-pending-identity-verification/509-5a435a5f-c0b9-4251-9ff9-34ba623b75ca.

494. **"infants":** McGreevy, Patrick. "California Unemployment Fraud

amid COVID-19 Pandemic May Total $2 Billion, Bank of America Says." *Los Angeles Times*, Dec. 7, 2020, www.latimes.com/california/story/2020-12-07/bank-of-america-estimate-2-billion-california-unemployment-fraud.

495. **"YouTube videos":** Letter from District Attorneys to Governor Gavin Newsom, "Re: Unemployment Insurance Fraud," Nov. 23, 2020, https://*CalMatters*.org/wp-content/uploads/2020/11/EDD-Letter.pdf.

496. **"criminal conduct":** Ibid.

497. "**David Chiu":** McGreevy, Patrick. "California's Prisoner Unemployment Fraud Now Estimated at $400 Million, Officials Say." *Los Angeles Times*, Dec. 1., 2020, www.latimes.com/california/story/2020-12-01/california-prisoner-unemployment-fraud-estimated-400-million.

498. **"zero-sum":** Letter to Governor Newsom, "Re: Unemployment Insurance Fraud."

499. **"done enough":** Venteicher, Wes, and David Lightman. "Murderers, Rapists Got Unemployment Money in Massive $1 Billion California Taxpayer Fraud." *Sacramento Bee*, Nov. 24, 2020. www.sacbee.com/news/california/article247397975.html.

500. **"asked and implored":** "EDD Scam: Serial Killers, Rapists, Murderers Claim COVID-Related Unemployment, District Attorneys Say." *KCRA*, Nov. 25, 2020, www.kcra.com/article/edd-scam-california-inmates-claim-over-dollar1b-in-covid-related-unemployment/34774966.

501. **"not cross-checking":** Gonzalez, Vicki. "EDD Fraud Involving California Inmates: 6 Things to Know about the Massive Scam." *KCRA*, Nov. 25, 2020, www.kcra.com/article/6-things-to-know-about-edd-fraud-involving-california-inmates/34779405.

502. **"slow and nonexistent":** Venteicher and Lightman.

503. **"Lisa A. Smittcamp":** Lightman, David, and Dale Kasler. "Feds Warned California This Spring That New Jobless Program Could Face Trouble with Fraud." *Sacramento Bee*, Dec. 3, 2020, www.sacbee.com/news/california/article247556175.html.

504. **"Michael Hestrin":** Kasler, Dale, and David Lightman. "COVID-19 Unemployment Scam Could Hit $2 Billion, Bank Tells California Lawmakers." *Sacramento Bee*, Dec. 7, www.sacbee.com/article247676875.html.

505. **"letter":** Lightman and Kasler. "Feds Warned California." www.sacbee.com/news/california/article247556175.html.

506. **"Cottie Petrie-Norris":** Skelton, George, "Newsom Endures Two Embarrassments with French Laundry Dinner and Unemployment Scam." *Los Angeles Times,* Dec. 3, 2020, www.latimes.com/california/story/2020-12-03/skelton-edd-inmate-unemployment-fraud-scandal-french-laundry-embarassment.

507. **"did not respond":** Taxin, Amy. "Official: California Fixed Glitch That Backlogged COVID Data." *Associated Press*, Aug. 8, 2020, apnews.com/article/san-francisco-virus-outbreak-california-8394ecef9fa842b6d89924c8acb21785.

508. **"We apologize":** Ibid.

509. **"Ghaly":** Ibid.

510. **"flying blind":** Ibid.

511. "**days before":** Luna, Taryn. "California Vows to Fix Coronavirus Reporting System amid Huge Backlog of Unreported Tests." *Los Angeles Times*, Aug. 7, 2020, www.latimes.com/california/story/2020-08-07/california-coronavirus-reporting-backlog-cases.

512. **"abruptly resigned."** Hoeven, Emily. "Sonia Angell, California's Public Health Director, Resigns." *CalMatters*, Aug. 10, 2020, *CalMatters*.org/newsletters/whatmatters/2020/08/sonia-angell-resigns-department-of-public-health-newsom/.

513. **"personnel matter":** "California Governor Gavin Newsom August 10 Press Conference Transcript." *Rev*, www.rev.com/blog/transcripts/california-governor-gavin-newsom-august-10-press-conference-transcript.

514. **"Associated Press":** Ibid.

515. **"investigation":** Zavala, Ashley. "California Lawmakers Want Oversight Hearing into COVID-19 Data Reporting Glitch." *FOX40*, Aug. 12, 2020, fox40.com/news/california-connection/california-lawmakers-want-oversight-hearing-into-covid-19-data-reporting-glitch/.

516. **"self-investigation":** Martichoux, Alix. "COVID Data Glitch Resulted in 300,000 Unprocessed Records, California Health Secretary Says." *ABC7 Los Angeles*, Aug. 7, 2020, abc7.com/health/covid-california-data-glitch-resulted-in-300k-unprocessed-records/6360234/.

517. **"rolling blackouts":** "California Governor Gavin Newsom August 17 Press Conference Transcript." *Rev*, www.rev.com/blog/transcripts/california-governor-gavin-newsom-august-17-press-conference-transcript.

518. **"not informed":** "Governor Newsom Demands Probe of Power Blackouts." *Associated Press*, Aug. 17, 2020, https://gooddaysacramento.cbslocal.com/2020/08/17/governor-newsom-probe-power-blackouts/.

519. **"failed to anticipate":** Kiley, Kevin. "Cross-Examining the Newsom Administration." *Capitol Quagmire*, https://blog.electkevinkiley.com/cross-examining-the-newsom-administration-8/.

520. **"false COVID data":** Kiley, Kevin. "Cross-Examining the Newsom Administration." *Capitol Quagmire*, https://blog.electkevinkiley.com/cross-examining-the-newsom-administration-7/

521. **"vaguely alluded":** "New Director Appointed to Lead California Employment Development Department." *Associated Press*, Dec. 31, 2020, www.latimes.com/california/story/2020-12-30/new-director-appointed-to-lead-california-employment-development-department.

Chapter 9: Partisan

522. **"Today":** Newsom, Gavin. *Twitter,* Jan. 3, 2020, https://twitter.com/GavinNewsom/status/1213138015343693825.

523. **"brief tribute":** Newsom, Gavin. *Twitter,* Sept. 18, 2020, https://twitter.

com/GavinNewsom/status/1307105403684167681.

524. **"four minutes":** Newsom, Gavin. *Twitter,* Sept. 18, 2020, https://twitter.com/GavinNewsom/status/1307106475794403331.

525. **"VOTE":** Newsom, Gavin. *Twitter,* Oct. 24, 2020, https://twitter.com/GavinNewsom/status/1320103294014943234.

526. **"sprinkled":** Newsom, Gavin. *Twitter,* Feb. 1, 2020, https://twitter.com/GavinNewsom/status/1223632914312765442.

527. **"South Carolina":** Newsom, Gavin. *Twitter,* Nov. 1, 2020, https://twitter.com/GavinNewsom/status/1322935041828139008.

528. **"27 times":** Newsom, Gavin. *Twitter,* search: McConnell from Jan. 1, 2019 to Dec. 31, 2019, https://twitter.com/search?q=McConnell%20(from%3AGavinNewsom)&src=typed_query&f=live.

529. **"sicken me":** Ibid.

530. **"ashamed":** Ibid.

531. **"cowardice":** Ibid.

532. **"Democratic Governor":** Ibid.

533. **"nine":** Ibid.

534. **"soulless inaction":** Ibid.

535. **"out of a job":** Ibid.

536. **"invertebrates":** Ibid.

537. **"step further":** Newsom, Gavin. *Twitter,* Oct. 12, 2020, https://twitter.com/GavinNewsom/status/1315793435035459584.

538. **"significant victory":** Myers, John. "Judge Rejects California Attorney General's Effort to Investigate GOP Ballot Boxes." *Los Angeles Times,* Oct, 21, 2020, www.latimes.com/california/story/2020-10-21/judge-rejects-california-attorney-general-investigation-gop-ballot-boxes.

539. **"Alex Padilla":** Korte, Lara. "California Owes $34 Million on a Voter Outreach Contract It Can't Pay For." *Sacramento Bee,* Dec. 4, 2020, www.

sacbee.com/news/politics-government/capitol-alert/article247538215.html.

540. **"Betty Yee":** "Betty Yee Must Uphold Law, Let Alex Padilla Clean up $35 Million Voter Contract Mess." *Sacramento Bee*, Nov. 24, 2020, www.sacbee.com/opinion/editorials/article247389635.html.

541. **"still made":** "Alex Padilla Senate Pick Makes History but Leaves California with $34 Million Bill." *Sacramento Bee*, Dec. 22, 2020, www.sacbee.com/opinion/editorials/article248032375.html.

542. "**politicization":** Ibid.

543. "partisan-tinged scandal": "California Must Cancel Secretive Voter Outreach Contract with Firm Linked to Biden." *Sacramento Bee*, Sept. 30. 2020. www.sacbee.com/opinion/editorials/article246101220.html.

544. **"Lindsay Graham":** Newsom, Gavin. *Twitter,* Sept. 19, 2020, https://twitter.com/GavinNewsom/status/1307335262318460929.

545. **"Mitch McConnell":** Newsom, Gavin. *Twitter,* Oct. 27, 2020, https://twitter.com/GavinNewsom/status/1321251237770088448.

546. **"Barrett":** archive.today webpage capture, https://archive.is/8D0Xv.

547. **"fake news":** Tash, Debra. "Gov. Newsom Falsely Suggests Barrett Once Opposed Tipping Court's Balance Of Power During An Election Year." *Citizens Journal*, Sept. 28, 2020, www.citizensjournal.us/gov-newsom-falsely-suggests-barrett-once-opposed-tipping-courts-balance-of-power-during-an-election-year/.

548. **"delete":** Ibid.

549. **"demean":** Newsom, Gavin. *Twitter,* Oct. 15, 2020, https://twitter.com/gavinnewsom/status/1316828036122124289?lang=en.

550. **"complimentary statements":** "California Gov. Newsom Finds New Friend in Washington: Trump." *Associated Press*, Apr. 23, 2020, www.usnews.com/news/best-states/washington/articles/2020-04-23/california-gov-newsom-finds-new-friend-in-washington-trump.

551. **"Devin Nunes":** "Gov. Gavin Newsom on How He's Handling

California's Outbreak." *The View*, YouTube, Apr. 3, 2020, https://www.youtube.com/watch?v=dJd6bGfLKXk

552. **"spurious chart":** Newsom, Gavin. *Twitter,* Oct. 22, 2020, https://twitter.com/GavinNewsom/status/1319449662533685250.

553. **"screenshot":** Dan Goodspeed. "Dan's COVID Charts Home," dangoodspeed.com/covid/.

554. **"reiterated":** CNBC Fast Money, *Facebook,* May 19, 2020, https://www.facebook.com/watch/?v=739612063246561.

555. **"opinion polls":** Lauter, David. "Californians Broadly Trust State Government on Coronavirus – but Mistrust Trump, Poll Finds." *Los Angeles Times*, May 1, 2020, www.latimes.com/politics/story/2020-05-01/partisan-split-coronavirus-newsom-approval-poll.

556. **"police powers":** Kiley, "Trial Documents in Gallagher and Kiley v. Newsom."

557. **"progressive goals":** Kiley, "Overview of Governor Gavin Newsom's Executive Action."

558. **"come to pass":** "Berman Bill Would Make Recent Election Reforms Permanent." Assembly Democratic Caucus, Press Release, Dec. 8. 2020, asmdc.org/press-releases/berman-bill-would-make-recent-election-reforms-permanent.

559. **"grandiose statements":** Office of Governor Gavin Newsom. "Governor Newsom Issues Executive Order to Protect Public Health by Mailing Every Registered Voter a Ballot Ahead of the November General Election." Press Release, May 8, 2020, www.gov.ca.gov/2020/05/08/governor-newsom-issues-executive-order-to-protect-public-health-by-mailing-every-registered-voter-a-ballot-ahead-of-the-november-general-election/.

560. **"Steyer Commission":** "Governor Newsom Taps California Business, Labor, Health Care and Community Leaders."

561. **"Joe Biden":** Biden, Joe. *Twitter,* Nov. 7, 2020, https://twitter.com/JoeBiden/status/1325118992785223682.

562. **"Good morning":** Newsom, Gavin. *Twitter,* Nov.5, 2020, https://twitter.com/GavinNewsom/status/1324373973149253632.

563. **"Trump supporters":** Sklar, Debbie L. "Ex-San Diego Mayor Kevin Faulconer Joins Effort to Recall Gov. Gavin Newsom." *Times of San Diego*, Jan. 3, 2021, timesofsandiego.com/politics/2021/01/02/ex-san-diego-mayor-kevin-faulconer-joins-effort-to-recall-gov-gavin-newsom/.

564. **"Willie Brown":** Brown, Willie. "Gavin Newsom Is in Trouble. Here's How He Can Survive." *San Francisco Chronicle*, Dec. 19, 2020, www.sfchronicle.com/bayarea/williesworld/article/Willie-Brown-Gavin-Newsom-is-in-trouble-15815052.php.

Chapter 10: Hypocritical

565. **"Gary Herbert":** NPR, Laurel Wamsley /. "Utah Gov. Announces Statewide Mask Mandate, Citing Steep Spike In COVID-19 Cases." *KPBS Public Media*, Nov. 9, 2020, www.kpbs.org/news/2020/nov/09/utah-gov-announces-statewide-mask-mandate-citing/#:~:text=%22Masks%20do%20not%20negatively%20affect,law%20that%20protects%20that%20freedom.%22.

566. **"opposition":** Romo, Diego. "Protest against Mask Requirements Held at Utah Capitol." *KSTU*, Oct. 25, 2020, www.fox13now.com/news/coronavirus/local-coronavirus-news/protest-against-mask-requirements-held-at-utah-capitol.

567. **"Simply put":** Willon, Phil et al. "Californians Must Wear Face Masks in Public under Coronavirus Order Issued by Newsom." *Los Angeles Times*, June 18, 2020, www.latimes.com/california/story/2020-06-18/california-mandatory-face-masks-statewide-order-coronavirus-gavin-newsom.

568. **"Don't be selfish":** Newsom, Gavin. *Twitter,* June 26, https://twitter.com/GavinNewsom/status/1276606160666103808.

569. **"again":** Newsom, Gavin. *Twitter,* July 16, https://twitter.com/GavinNewsom/status/1283841170590674945.

570. **"not mentioned":** Newsom, Gavin. *Twitter*, search: mask or masks, https://twitter.com/search?q=(mask%20OR%20masks)%20(from%3AGavinNewsom)&src=typed_query&f=live.

571. **"Rhode Island":** "Governor to Require Masks When in Public; RI Adds 241 Cases." *U.S. News & World Report*, May 5, 2020, www.usnews.com/news/best-states/rhode-island/articles/2020-05-05/police-break-up-several-large-groups-fbi-joins-fraud-probe.

572. **"WEAR A MASK":** Newsom, Gavin. *Twitter*, search mask or masks https://twitter.com/search?q=(mask%20OR%20masks)%20(from%3AGavinNewsom)&src=typed_query&f=live.

573. **"Lowercase versions":** Ibid.

574. **"most exclusive":** White, Jeremy B. "Newsom Faces Backlash after Attending French Laundry Dinner Party." *Politico*, Nov. 13, 2020, www.politico.com/states/california/story/2020/11/13/newsom-faces-backlash-after-attending-french-laundry-dinner-party-1336419.

575. **"National Registry":** "Search." National Parks Service, U.S. Department of the Interior, npgallery.nps.gov/NRHP.

576. **"Top 50":** "The World's 50 Best Restaurants: The Best Restaurants in the World,." www.theworlds50best.com/.

577. **"three-Michelin-star":** Repanich, Jeremy. "Here Are the 14 US Restaurants Rated 3 Stars by Michelin in 2020." *Robb Report*, Oct. 28, 2019, robbreport.com/food-drink/dining/us-3-michelin-star-restaurants-sf-ny-chi-dc-eg18-2832537/.

578. **"Thomas Keller":** Keller., Thomas. "Honors & Accolades," www.thomaskeller.com/yountville-california/thomas-keller/honors-accolades.

579. **"same ingredient":** Keller, Thomas. "Today's Menus," www.thomaskeller.com/new-york-new-york/per-se/todays-menus.

580. **"contemporary American":** "The BEST Restaurant in the World, No Really." *Shades of Pinck*, Aug. 5, 2016, shadesofpinck.com/the-best-restaurant-in-the-world-no-really-the-french-laundry/.

581. **"the Onion":** Mehendale, Nick. "Gavin Newsom Slammed For Eating At The French Laundry When Atelier Crenn Clearly Superior Take On Contemporary Cuisine." *The Onion*, Nov. 19, 2020, www.theonion.com/gavin-newsom-slammed-for-eating-at-the-french-laundry-w-1845716527.

582. **"50th birthday":** Koseff, Alexei. "Newsom Attended French Laundry Party with More Households than California Advises during Pandemic." *San Francisco Chronicle*, Nov. 14, 2020, www.sfchronicle.com/politics/article/Newsom-attended-French-Laundry-party-with-more-15725393.php.

583. **"other lobbyists":** White, Jeremy B. and Victoria Colliver. "California Doctors' Top Brass Attended French Laundry Dinner with Newsom." *Politico*, Nov. 18, 2020, www.politico.com/states/california/story/2020/11/18/california-medical-association-brass-attended-french-laundry-dinner-with-newsom-kinney-1336924.

584. **"Photographs":** Melugin, Bill. "FOX 11 Obtains Exclusive Photos of Gov. Newsom at French Restaurant Allegedly Not Following COVID-19 Protocols." *FOX 11 Los Angeles*, Nov. 19, 2020, www.foxla.com/news/fox-11-obtains-exclusive-photos-of-gov-newsom-at-french-restaurant-allegedly-not-following-covid-19-protocols.

585. **"wine bill":** Brown, Willie. "Newsom Only Hurt Himself by Attending Fancy Restaurant Party." *San Francisco Chronicle*, Nov. 21, 2020, www.sfchronicle.com/bayarea/williesworld/article/Willie-Brown-Newsom-only-hurt-himself-by-15743668.php.

586. **"Gatsby-esque":** Pawel, Miriam. "Gavin Newsom, What Were You Thinking?" *New York Times*, Nov. 25, 2020, www.nytimes.com/2020/11/25/opinion/gavin-newsom-french-laundry-california.html.

587. **"the noise":** Melguin and Insheiwat

588. **"story headlined":** Fuller, Thomas. "For California Governor the Coronavirus Message Is Do as I Say, Not as I Dine." *New York Times*, Nov. 18, 2020, www.nytimes.com/2020/11/18/us/newsom-california-covid-french-laundry.html.

589. **"launder the stain":** "Gavin Newsom's Hypocritical French Laundry

Fiasco Harms California's COVID-19 Efforts." *Sacramento Bee*, Nov. 13, 2020, www.sacbee.com/opinion/editorials/article247181176.html.

590. **"layers":** Ibid.

591. **"next press conference":** Skelton, George. "Newsom Endures Two Embarrassments with French Laundry Dinner and Unemployment Scam." *Los Angeles Times*, Dec. 3, 2020, www.latimes.com/california/story/2020-12-03/skelton-edd-inmate-unemployment-fraud-scandal-french-laundry-embarassment.

592. **"safety precautions":** Woodrow, Melanie. "Gov. Newsom Says He Shouldn't Have Attended Birthday Party at French Laundry amid COVID-19 Surge." *ABC7 San Francisco*, Nov. 14, 2020, abc7news.com/gavin-newsom-party-french-laundry-coronavirus-gathering-guidelines-birthday/7931674/.

593. **"photos":** Melguin and Insheiwat.

594. **"guidance":** "California Gov. Gavin Newsom Encourages Wearing Masks between Bites While Eating." *KHQ Right Now*, Oct. 9, 2020, www.khq.com/news/california-gov-gavin-newsom-encourages-wearing-masks-between-bites-while-eating/article_7d03d376-0a5c-11eb-8ee7-e39653b2443f.html.

595. **"animation":** Newsom, Gavin. *Twitter,* Mar. 25, 2020. https://twitter.com/GavinNewsom/status/1242965263856717825.

596. **"Tom Steyer":** "How Tom Steyer Is Advising Gov. Newsom on California's Economic Recovery during Pandemic." *KCRW*, Aug. 20, 2020, www.kcrw.com/news/shows/press-play-with-madeleine-brand/election-2020-ridesharing-coronavirus-economy-friendship/tom-steyer-econ-covid-19-task-force.

597. **"cannot continue":** "Governor Gavin Newsom June 24 California Press Conference Transcript." *Rev*, www.rev.com/blog/transcripts/governor-gavin-newsom-june-24-california-press-conference-transcript.

598. **"cell phone data":** Koop, Chacour. "Is California Staying Home? Here's What GPS Phone Data Say in Coronavirus Pandemic." *Sacramento Bee*, Apr.

9, 2020, www.sacbee.com/news/coronavirus/article241905751.html.

599. **"Rob Stutzman":** Skelton, "Newsom Endures."

600. **"reliable paycheck":** "Comparison of State Legislative Salaries." *Ballotpedia*, ballotpedia.org/Comparison_of_state_legislative_salaries#:~:text=In%20California%2C%20legislators%20are%20paid%20%24110%2C459%20per%20year%20in%20salary..

601. **"special DMV":** Anderson, Bryan. "'Secret' DMV Office Serving California Lawmakers Would Be Closed under GOP Proposal." *Sacramento Bee*, Apr. 4, 2019, www.sacbee.com/news/politics-government/capitol-alert/article228840304.html.

602. **"junkets":** "California Lawmakers, Lavish Junkets Are Burning Your Constituents." *The Desert Sun*, Jan. 10, 2019, www.desertsun.com/story/opinion/editorials/2019/01/10/california-lawmaker-lavish-junkets-burn-constituents-desert-sun-editorial-board/2529551002/.

603. **"sent his kids":** Mays, Mackenzie. "Newsom Sends His Children Back to Private School Classrooms in California." *Politico*, Oct. 30, 2020, www.politico.com/states/california/story/2020/10/30/newsom-sends-his-children-back-to-school-classrooms-in-california-1332811.

604. **"column subtitled":** Pawel, "Gavin Newsom, What Were You Thinking?"

605. **"utopia":** Orr, Katie. "California Lawmakers Approve $200 Billion State Budget." *KQED*, June 15, 2018, www.kqed.org/news/11674996/california-lawmakers-approve-200-billion-state-budget.

606. **"Edwin Lombard":** "Statement by Edwin Lombard."

607. **"Black lives":** Ibid.

608. **"my colleagues":** "We Have a Legislature That Isn't Run by Legislators." YouTube, YouTube, July 4, 2020, www.youtube.com/watch?v=KJtsKk3NMYM.

609. **"turned to their remarks":** Ibid.

Chapter 11: Neglectful

610. **"victory lap":** "CA Gov: All Governors Should Issue Stay at Home Orders Now, What Are They Waiting for? *CNN*, Apr. 1., 2020, www.cnn.com/videos/tv/2020/04/01/lead-gov-gavin-newsom-live-jake-tapper.cnn.
611. **"message":** Ibid.
612. **"testing backlog":** Ibid.
613. **"major new initiative":** Office of Governor Gavin Newsom. "Governor Newsom Announces California Health Corps, a Major Initiative to Expand Health Care Workforce to Fight COVID-19." Press Release, Mar. 31, 2020, www.gov.ca.gov/2020/03/30/governor-newsom-announces-california-health-corps-a-major-initiative-to-expand-health-care-workforce-to-fight-covid-19/.
614. **"37,000-plus": "**Gov. Gavin Newsom of California COVID-19 Press Conference Transcript March 30." *Rev*, 6 May 2020, www.rev.com/blog/transcripts/gov-gavin-newsom-of-california-covid-19-press-conference-transcript-march-30.
615. **"initial results":** "California Gov. Gavin Newsom COVID-19 Briefing April 7." *Rev*, 6 May 2020, www.rev.com/blog/transcripts/california-gov-gavin-newsom-covid-19-briefing-april-7.
616. **"94,000":** Gutierrez, Melody. "California Health Officials Scramble to Staff Medical Facilities amid COVID-19 Surge." *Los Angeles Times*, Dec. 16. 2020, www.latimes.com/california/story/2020-12-15/california-health-officials-scramble-covid-19-surge-locations-staffing.
617. **"heroes":** Office of Governor Gavin Newsom. "Governor Newsom Announces California Health Corps, a Major Initiative to Expand Health Care Workforce to Fight COVID-19." Press Release, Mar. 31, 2020, www.gov.ca.gov/2020/03/30/governor-newsom-announces-california-health-corps-a-major-initiative-to-expand-health-care-workforce-to-fight-covid-19/.

618. **"out of capacity":** "'Health Corps': Gov. Newsom Wanted Retired Doctors and Nurses to Help Treat COVID Patients. What Happened?" *KCRW*, Dec. 8, 2020, www.kcrw.com/news/shows/press-play-with-madeleine-brand/coronavirus-resistance-retired-health-workers-stock-market-film/health-corps-gavin-newsom-covid-19.

619. **"21 of them":** Gutierrez, "California Health Officials Scramble."

620. **"perfect":** KCRW, "Health Corps."

621. **"investigative report":** Pohl, Jason. "Newsom Asked California Doctors and Nurses to Join His Health Corps. Why the Plan Flopped." *Sacramento Bee*, Dec. 1, 2020, www.sacbee.com/news/coronavirus/article247508320.html#:~:text=Gavin%20Newsom%20announced%20the%20creation,professionals%20into%20COVID%2D19%20hotspots.

622. **"Stephanie Roberson":** Ibid.

623. **"fanfare":** Gutierrez

624. **"a few applicants":** Pohl

625. **"haphazard scheduling":** Ibid.

626. **"at the mercy":** Ibid

627. **"constituents":** Gallagher, James. *Twitter,* search: health, https://twitter.com/search?q=Health%20(from%3AJ_GallagherAD3)&src=typed_query&f=live

628. **"ineligible":** "Most Enlistees Not Eligible to Join California Health Corps." *Associated Press*, May 1, 2020, www.usnews.com/news/politics/articles/2020-05-01/most-california-health-corps-volunteers-not-eligible-to-join.

629. **"staffing ratios":** Rivera, Author: Kurt. "California Nurses Push Back against New Nurse to Patient Ratios during Covid-19 Pandemic." *abc10*, Dec. 17, 2020, www.abc10.com/article/news/health/coronavirus/california-nurses-patient-ratio/103-494ece17-1818-43d4-82c0-58dfa68197cf.

630. **"nursing students":** Smith, Ashley A. "Nursing Students Are Eager to

Answer California's Call to Help Stop Coronavirus Spread." *EdSource*, Mar. 26, 2020, edsource.org/2020/nursing-students-are-eager-to-answer-californias-call-to-help-stop-coronavirus-spread/627175.

631. **"renewed calls":** Gutierrez

632. **"dusting that off":** Pohl

633. **"Tracking Project":** Woolfolk, John. "Report: California Has Third-Lowest U.S. Coronavirus Testing Rate." *Mercury News*, Apr. 21, 2020, www.mercurynews.com/2020/04/20/report-california-has-third-lowest-u-s-coronavirus-testing-rate/.

634. **"Stephen Morrison":** Ibid.

635. **"I tried":** Kiley, Kevin. *Twitter,* Apr. 23, https://twitter.com/KevinKileyCA/status/1253364398241923072.

636. **"task force":** Woolfolk.

637. **"short supply":** "California Health Care Leaders Respond to New COVID-19 Testing Guidance." Cmadocs, www.cmadocs.org/newsroom/news/view/ArticleId/48968/California-health-care-leaders-respond-to-Newsom-Administration-s-new-COVID-19-testing-guidance.

638. **"conduct tests":** Dizikes, Cynthia. "California's Pharmacies Haven't Tested for Coronavirus, Unlike in Other States." *San Francisco Chronicle*, May 2, 2020, www.sfchronicle.com/bayarea/article/Why-California-won-t-enlist-its-6-300-15241712.php.

639. **"swab-and-send":** "Governor of California Signs Executive Order Permitting Pharmacists, Pharmacy Technicians to Conduct CLIA-Waived COVID-19 Tests." *Pharmacy Times*, Aug. 26, 2020, www.pharmacytimes.com/news/governor-of-california-signs-executive-order-permitting-pharmacists-pharmacy-technicians-to-conduct-clia-waived-covid-19-tests.

640. **"6-to-1 ratio":** Silver, Nate. *Twitter,* Apr. 22, https://twitter.com/NateSilver538/status/1253018928034590721.

641. **"New York":** Silver, Nate. *Twitter,* Apr. 22, https://twitter.com/NateSilver538/status/1253017964082860032.

642. **"testing situation":** Ibid.

643. **"worst data":** Silver, Nate. *Twitter,* Apr. 22, https://twitter.com/NateSilver538/status/1253167085213138944.

644. **"such a mess":** Silver, Nate. *Twitter,* Apr. 22, https://twitter.com/NateSilver538/status/1253168184598855690.

645. **"substantial lags":** Silver, Nate. *Twitter,* Apr. 22, https://twitter.com/NateSilver538/status/1253075321244520448.

646. **"Lee Riley":** Melley, "Once a Model."

647. "**lagging behind":** Money, Luke et al. "California's Vaccine Rollout Has Been Too Slow, Newsom Says, with Only 35% of Doses Administered." *Los Angeles Times*, Jan. 4, 2021, www.latimes.com/california/story/2021-01-04/newsom-california-covid-vaccine-rollout-too-slow.

648. **"too slow":** Ibid.

649. **"Mike Wasserman":** Ibid.

650. **"deaths":** "Tracking the Coronavirus in California Nursing Homes." *Los Angeles Times*, Jan. 9, 2021, www.latimes.com/projects/california-coronavirus-cases-tracking-outbreak/nursing-homes/.

651. **"testing":** "Why Nursing Homes Become COVID-19 Hot Spots." *California Health Care Foundation*, Aug. 12, 2020, www.chcf.org/blog/why-nursing-homes-become-covid-19-hot-spots/#:~:text=%E2%80%9CTo%20keep%20the%20virus%20out,within%20minutes%2C%20not%20days.%E2%80%9D.

652. **"short staffed":** Ibid.

653. **"outrage":** Luna, Taryn. "Criticism Grows."

654. **"discriminatory":** Ibid.

655. **"quietly":** Ibid.

656. **"failed":** Pawel, "Gavin Newsom, What Were You Thinking?"

657. **"121 inmates":** Egelko, Bob. "San Quentin Must Release or Transfer

Half Its Prisoners Because of Lack of COVID Care, Court Rules." *San Francisco Chronicle*, Oct. 21, 2020, www.sfchronicle.com/bayarea/article/San-Quentin-must-release-or-transfer-half-its-15662794.php.

658. **"Thirty employees":** "First San Quentin State Prison Employee Dies From Coronavirus," patch.com/california/millvalley/first-san-quentin-state-prison-employee-dies-coronavirus.

659. **"deliberate indifference":** Thompson, Don. "Court Orders California to Cut San Quentin Inmates by Half." *Associated Press*, Oct. 22, 2020, apnews.com/article/pandemics-virus-outbreak-san-francisco-prisons-california-b8838a67b75c415322e2f182c79c106c.

660. **"Marc Levine":** Assemblymember Marc Levine. "Assemblymember Levine Releases Statement from Senate Public Safety Committee Hearing on CDCR Failures at San Quentin State Prison," Press Release, July 1, 2020, a10.asmdc.org/press-releases/20200701-assemblymember-levine-releases-statement-senate-public-safety-committee.

661. **"respectfully disagreed":** Sze, Kristen. "California Court of Appeals Orders 50% Population Reduction at San Quentin Prison." *ABC7 San Francisco*, Oct. 21, 2020, abc7news.com/san-quentin-prison-coronavirus-outbreak-inmates-covid-hadar-aviram/7198733/.

662. **"worst in nation":** Hwang and Buchmann.

Chapter 12: Back to Basics

663. **"leadership":** Pawel, "What Were You Thinking, Gavin Newsom?"

664. "**1,039 homeless":** Goodheart

665. **"growing faster":** Oreskes, Benjamin, "California Has the Most Homeless People of Any State. But L.A. Is Still a National Model." *Los Angeles Times*, Aug. 1, 2019, www.latimes.com/california/story/2019-08-01/california-homeless-people-housing-national-model-conference.

666. **"Legislative Analyst":** Cahill, Nick. "California's Legislative Analyst Spots Potential Pitfalls in Governor's Homelessness Plan." *CNS*, Feb. 12, 2020, www.courthousenews.com/californias-legislative-analyst-spots-potential-pitfalls-in-governors-homelessness-plan/.

667. **"$1.4 billion":** Myers, John and Doug Smith. "Gov. Gavin Newsom Calls for $1.4 Billion in New Help for Homeless." *Los Angeles Times*, Jan. 8, 2020, www.latimes.com/california/story/2020-01-08/gavin-newsom-california-homeless-help-budget.

668. **"full audit":** Letter from Kevin Kiley to Rudy Salas, Jan. 13. 2020, https://jones.cssrc.us/sites/default/files/200114_HomelessnessAuditRequest.pdf.

669. **"abstain":** Joint Legislative Audit Committee, Roll Call/Voting Form, Feb. 26, 2020, https://legaudit.assembly.ca.gov/sites/legaudit.assembly.ca.gov/files/regular%20calendar%20votes_Feb26.pdf.

670. **"Jerry Brown":** Koseff, Alexei. "Gavin Newsom Wants to Redesign California's Tax System. It's so Hard, Jerry Brown Didn't Try." *Sacramento Bee*, Nov. 19, 2018, www.sacbee.com/news/politics-government/capitol-alert/article221751020.html.

Chapter 13: The Revival of Self-Government

671. **"Proposition 9":** Guynn, Jessica. "This Is Why Silicon Valley Venture Capitalist Tim Draper Wants to Break California into Three." *USA Today*, June 15, 2018, www.usatoday.com/story/tech/2018/06/13/california-three-states-ballot-tim-draper-interview-usa-today/699185002/.

672. **"Draper":** Ibid.

673. **"220 efforts":** to Library, California State. "Breaking Up California: A History of Many Attempts," www.library.ca.gov/collections/online-exhibits/splitting-ca/.

674. **"Healthy Communities":** Kiley, Kevin. "The Healthy Communities Resolution." *Capitol Quagmire,* https://blog.electkevinkiley.com/the-health-

communities-resolution-2/.

675. **"legislative districts":** Cullen, Morgan. "2010 Constituents Per State Legislative District Table," www.ncsl.org/research/about-state-legislatures/2010-constituents-per-state-legislative-district.aspx.

676. **"In these States":** 1 Alexis de Tocqueville, Democracy in America (John. C. Spencer Ed.), 270.

677. **"cares of political":** Ibid, 272.

678. **"trifling":** Ibid.

679. **"New England":** Ibid, 70.

680. **"political agitation":** Ibid, 271.

681. **"Athens":** Ostwald, Martin. "Shares and Rights: Citizenship Greek Style and American Style," Interpretations of the Western World. (Boston: Pearson Custom Publishing, 2004), 41

682. **"2018 study":** "Just One in Three Americans Can Pass the U.S. Citizenship Test Which Immigrants Must Take." *Daily Mail Online*, Oct. 5, 2018, www.dailymail.co.uk/news/article-6237009/Just-one-three-Americans-pass-U-S-Citizenship-Test-immigrants-take.html.

683. "**small step":** "How to Bolster the 1st Amendment on College Campuses," *Los Angeles Times*, Apr. 27, 2018, www.latimes.com/opinion/editorials/la-ed-campus-speech-20180427-story.html.

684. **"John Adams":** "John Adams Academies, Inc." Ten Core Values, roseville.johnadamsacademy.org/apps/pages/index.jsp?uREC_ID=2003858&type=d&pREC_ID=2094302.